Endorsements

"Dr. Mitzi Gold has written one of the best self-help books I have read in years. It puts happiness into the reader's hands, attitudes, and intentions. It reminds me of the Greek philosopher Epictetus who remarked, 'It is not what happens to us that is important, it is how we react to the event that is important.' He knew about the role of intention centuries ago, and his advice is spelled out in this life-changing book. Dr. Gold's Circle of Life process gives readers tools they need to transform their lives and feel grateful for the journey."

—Stanley Krippner, Ph.D. co-author *Personal Mythology*

"William James, the father of American psychology, said, "The transition from tenseness, self-responsibility, and worry, to equanimity, receptivity, and peace, is the most wonderful of all those shiftings of inner equilibrium . . . and the chief wonder of it is that it so often comes about, not by doing, but by simply relaxing and throwing the burden down." In *Balancing Your Circle of Life*, Dr. Mitzi Gold shows us how to unburden ourselves of negative habits and beliefs that limit our life's possibilities. If you are ready for greater joy, creativity, and fulfillment, this book is for you."

—Larry Dossey, M.D.
Author of *Healing Words, Reinventing Medicine,
The One Mind* and *One Mind: How Our Individual Mind Is
Part of a Greater Consciousness and Why It Matters*

"Dr. Gold's book is a blessing for anyone who wants to have a healthier, happier, longer, more fulfilled life."

—Patricia Bragg, N.D., Ph.D.

"A good self-help book has to stretch your envelope of possibility, lead you into asking new questions and exploring new areas, and help you organize what you do to achieve a clear goal. This book meets all these criteria and more. Dr. Gold has synthesized many years of work into a clear, inspiring and energizing package. She puts complex thoughts and insights into simple pathways for a book that can be more used than simply read."

—Dennis Jaffe, Ph.D. author of *Healing from Within*

"Our resilient and creative powers can open doors and bring new life options, if we are willing to look honestly and risk change. This engaging book offers both tools and stories so it can happen for us."

—Dr. Ruth Richards, Saybrook University, and Author/Editor, *Everyday Creativity* and *New Views of Human Nature*. (American Psychological Association, 2007)

"With a joyful positivity about life and change, grounded in decades of wisdom and experience, Dr. Gold beautifully guides you through a simple yet powerful process to transform all aspects of your life.

You will be amazed and inspired by how these practical steps lead you on a path to the life and relationships you truly want. Enjoy the process!

This book is a true gift to yourself, and to those you love."

—Warren Berland, Ph.D., author of *Out of the Box for Life: Being Free is Just a Choice* (HarperCollins)

Balancing Your Circle of Life

Create Your Lifestyle, Relationships and Happiness with Intention

Mitzi Gold
Ph.D., LCSW, MPH

Life Master Books™

Copyright © 2013, 2017 by Mitzi Gold

To make inquiries: www.lifemasterbooks.com
info@lifemasterbooks.com

Published by Life Master Books™

All rights reserved. No part of this book may be reproduced, stored in a retrieval system, or transmitted in any form or by any means, electronic, mechanical, photocopying, recording, or otherwise, without prior written permission of the publisher. To make inquiries: info@drmitzigold.com or visit, marsvenushawaii.com

ISBN: 978-0-9858231-0-8 (paperback)
ISBN: 978-0-9858231-1-5 (ebook / ePub)
ISBN: 978-0-9858231-2-2 (ebook / Kindle & Mobi)

Get the right digital edition for your favorite eReader: Get the ePub for iPads and B&N Nook, and Mobi for Kindle and the Sony eReader.

Cover photo: ©istockphoto.com/quintanilla. The cover design incorporates an Enso painted by Andy Kay. One Enso holds the ocean and sky, representing all of nature. The other Enso surrounds the woman and the possibility of what will be created as she moves through her life. This symbolizes the idea of "all there is and all that will be." "The Enso is the circle of infinity, symbol of simplicity with profundity, emptiness with fullness, the visible and invisible . . . although the shape is the simplest imaginable, each circle is different."
—*Sacred Calligraphy of the East* by John Stevens

Author photo: Palladino/Den Photography

Bookcover and page design by DesignForBooks.com

Important Caution: Please read this

DISCLAIMER

This book contains the opinions and ideas of the author. Intended to provide helpful and informative material on the subject matter covered, it is offered with the express understanding that the author is not your personal healthcare provider, nor is the author made so by your act of reading this book.

The author specifically disclaims all responsibility for any liability, loss, or risk, personal or otherwise that may be incurred as a consequence, direct or indirect, by the use or application of techniques and/or content in this book.

This book is intended for self-help and/or personal development. If you are presently seeing a healthcare provider, you may want to let him or her know you are reading it. Please seek professional help if you think you need it.

Dedicated to Frank Rogers, his constant love and support energizes my passion for living. His forward thinking, vision, and drive inspires me every day.

Acknowledgments

In deep appreciation and profound gratitude to the following special people for their generous support, inspiration, and presence in my evolving life.

Stanley Krippner, Ph.D., a foremost expert in multiple fields of academics—always insightful, resourceful, and wise. He is one of my most treasured mentors.

John Gray, Ph.D., who transformed my personal and professional life with his insights, deep understanding, and healing skills for men, women and their relationships. His passion for living a healthy life inspired me to share his wisdom with others.

Martin Seligman, Ph.D., a brilliant scholar who founded the field of Positive Psychology and taught me about the science of being happy.

Joseph Campbell, Ph.D., whose wisdom helped me identify and participate in my "heroine's journey."

Jean Shinoda Bolen, M.D., who introduced me to my inner goddesses and gods.

José Arguelles, Ph.D., whose seminal book "Mandala" captured my imagination and introduced me to mandalas and the power of symbols.

Randolph Stone, DO, DC, a remarkable teacher who introduced me to Polarity Therapy and encouraged me to be a teacher of energy principles. I received my Board Certification as a Polarity Practitioner (BCPP) in 2016.

Pierre Pannetier, ND, who taught me, by showing me, how to teach with love.

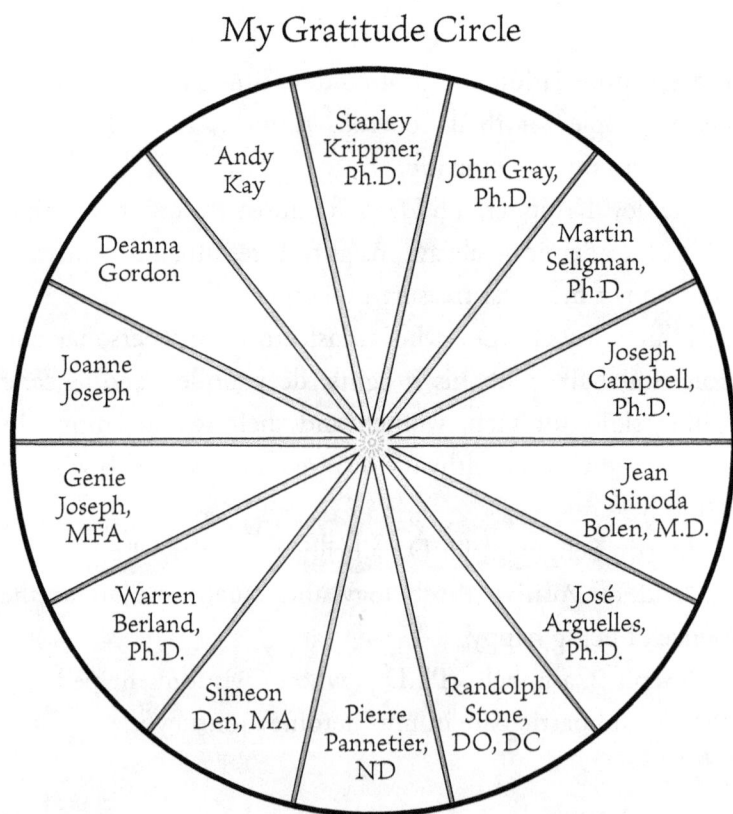

My Gratitude Circle

Simeon Den, MA, who always has inspired me to dance and whose friendship always makes me feel like I am dancing.

Warren Berland, Ph.D., ACSW, a serious and sincere coach whose bottom line is success.

Genie Joseph, MFA, Ph.D., my writing coach who kept me going to the finish line and made sharing my "Circle of Life" a joyful writing process.

Joanne Joseph, for her careful, attentive first proofing and editing.

Deanna Gordon, who was always enthusiastic and sincerely willing to find ways to enhance my book and bring it to the public.

Andy Kay, my delightful Zen brush painting teacher who introduced me to the magic of Enso's and dragons.

Further acknowledgement goes to the following colleagues for their enthusiasm for my project: David Paperny, Babs Clough, Cryslea Russell, Marti Barham, Evelyne Raposo, Meryn Callandar and Bobbie Burnett.

To my conscientious patients willing to create their Circle of Life and follow their self-designed paths to happiness.

To special family and friends for their belief in this project and sincere encouragement: The Graumann Family, Sirena Castillo Long, Alika Serrato, Vima Lamura, the Joseph Family, and to Rachael Angelese.

Thank you all for assisting in bringing this project to fruition.

In Memoriam

Big Bopper & Mom, who are dearly missed,
"Onward and Upward"

Contents

Foreword   xi

Introduction   xv

Part One

The Process of Creating Your Circle of Life

1 How to Get Started . . . The Six Small Steps to a Big Future   1
2 What Your Circle of Life Tells You about Your Life   11
3 Creating the Slices for Your Circle of Life   19
4 Using Your Outer Circle to Transform Your Life   39
5 How to Use Your Intention to Experience Desired Changes   51
6 Filling versus Emptying Your Circle   63

Part Two

Using Your Circle of Life Process to
Re-Design Your Future: The Skills You Need To Help
You Get the Most Out of Your Circle of Life

7 Using the Power of Affirmations to Change Your Behavior 71
8 Enhancing Your Self-Esteem to Create the Life of Your Dreams 79
9 Reclaiming Your Zest for Life through Creativity 87
10 Living Forward—Committing to Your Life's Journey 95
11 You're Circle of Life as an Upward Spiral 101

Part Three

Using The Circle of Life to Transform
Specific Areas of Your Life

12 The Circle of Love—The Couples Circle 109
13 The Importance of Self-Care 121
14 Creating Passion, Purpose, and Direction 129
15 Teen Circles—What's My Life All About? 137
16 Spirituality and Your Relationship to the Universe 149
17 The Life Review Circle 155
18 Conclusion 173

Recommended Reading and Further Resources 177
Draw Your Own Circle of Life 187
About the Author 203

Foreword

During thirty years as a therapist in private practice, I have seen many people come into my office wanting to change their life. They just don't know how to start. They feel confused, hopeless, and overwhelmed, without a clue as to where to begin. All they know is that they want to lead happier lives. For some people, even making the first step to seek professional help is a big deal, and I wanted to give them a tool that they could easily learn and quickly use. That's how I developed the Circle of Life process.

The Circle of Life process gives people the tools to make a realistic assessment of where their lives are right now, and what simple actions they can take to begin to make the changes that will be helpful. It is a starting point for taking control over one's life and crafting a future based on one's true desires.

After using the Circle of Life process for over twenty years with couples, individuals, and families, I am still impressed by the profound changes people can and do make in their lives using this simple process. The first steps give patients the opportunity to experience their present life as a whole, and then to design a path to create an inspiring future. The best part of the Circle of Life process is that no one is telling you what to do or even how to do it. You already know what is working or not working in your life. You are the one who decides what and how fast you want to change.

I created this book to give people a place to start to make the changes they desire, and also to give them a life-long tool. Keeping a book or file of all your Circles as you move through the important stages of life provides a wonderful resource that will inspire and assist you during challenging times. Seeing how much progress you have made will motivate you to keep going. Viewing your life span over the course of time can be amazing, if you choose to do the crucial Life Review process at the end of this book.

The Circle of Life process is basic enough for everyone. It is adjustable to the individual's level of development. It is simple enough for adolescents who want to set their lives on the right course. It is powerful enough to help adults navigate the twists and turns of opportunities and choices. The Couples Circle helps get relationships back on track and leads to more fulfilling partnerships. It is sophisticated enough for mature, conscious seekers to gain deep insight, and to make sure the second half of their lives is meaningful and pleasurable.

The Circle of Life encourages you to view your life as a creative process. Instead of focusing on what you think you did "wrong," you learn to focus on what you can do to get into the driver's seat of your life and move forward. It uses positive self-talk, creative imagination, affirmations, and simple action plans. As a therapist, I have always found it exciting to see how patients can use this process to quickly empower themselves to be the best they can be, and to live meaningful and enriched lives. I acknowledge and congratulate the efforts and amazing progress my patients have made using this process as they achieved their desires for personal development and success. I am also honored to play a role in your life's journey as well.

Life is about moving toward self mastery, and the Circle of Life process is the perfect tool to help you achieve all your goals. It will quickly lead you to more clarity, focus, and hope. I truly believe it will inspire you to live your life as you've always dreamed it could be.

—Mitzi Gold, Ph.D., LCSW, MPH, LMT, BCPP
Honolulu, Hawaii, 2012

"The circle is the simplest shape there is. When we brush a circle with ink on paper, we create an Enso. Each one is different. This celebration of uniqueness is mirrored in the Enso and shows the quality of energy of that person creating the Enso in that moment."

—Andy Kay
Andy Kay, Zen Brush Artist,
Enso Instructor

Introduction

Symbols are images that carry deep, profound meanings for the social groups that employ them, and the mandala is one of the most frequently encountered. From the Tibetan and Navajo circular sand mosaics to the wheels in ancient Vedic texts and Carl Jung's drawings in *The Red Book,* mandalas have been used to represent wholeness, closure, and a completed journey. Dr. Mitzi Gold has gifted her readers with two mandalas, one a "Circle of Life" and the other a "Life Review Circle." Both symbols emerged from Dr. Gold's three decades as a successful and highly creative psychotherapist and counselor, working with individuals and couples across the age span.

The first mandala allows readers to view their entire life as a circle, albeit one that is sliced into a dozen or more segments, each representing a life issue such as physical health, spirituality, or finance. The other mandala "pie" is divided into seven-year "pieces," permitting the reader a retrospective view.

In her psychotherapy sessions, Dr. Gold uses this process with her patients, and the readers of this book now have the tools to engage in this illuminating process on their own. Included also are useful case histories that demonstrate how practical utilizations of common sense, judgment, insight, and intuition can evoke desired life changes.

Many readers will find the exercises so useful that they will reconstruct these mandalas whenever life's challenges require a thoughtful response rather than a knee-jerk reaction. If these twin mandalas are approached with mindfulness and carried out in a contemplative manner, Dr. Gold's readers may wake up some morning and happily find themselves transformed.

—Stanley Krippner, Ph.D.
Alan Watts Professor of Psychology,
Saybrook University, San Francisco, CA

Part One

The Process
of Creating
Your Circle of Life

CHAPTER 1

How to Get Started

It's All a Circle of Life

Welcome to right now! This present moment may not fit your picture of *perfect*—but one good thing about this moment is that it is the perfect time for change. The present is your most powerful time frame, because the future gets better by making even small changes in the present. It all begins by taking an honest look at how things really are going right now in your present life. When you are willing to simply look at how things really are in your life right now, your attention moves into the present. Focusing on the present moves you out of worry about the future, and away from fixation on the past. By just looking at what is so in your life without judgment, you can begin to see what is working and what isn't working. Then you can make some decisions about what you really want to change.

Some people think that ignoring what isn't working in their life is preferable to facing the parts that feel "broken."

Ignoring the parts of ourselves that we find unacceptable only increases their influence in our lives. Rather than diminishing their impact, ignoring the things that aren't working can lead to feelings of being trapped, stuck, and hopeless. Sometimes just facing the things that you have been avoiding—and owning and accepting that they are so—is the first step to liberation. In this way, the Circle of Life process can be a wonderfully revealing approach that helps us see aspects of ourselves that we may have repressed or suppressed.

As you take the first steps to accepting the parts of yourself you haven't owned, a magical process unfolds. Accepting your "shadow side" leads to a whole new integration. We all have a shadow, which is simply that part of ourselves that we have forgotten, ignored, denied, or overlooked. Sometimes the shadow is composed of negative traits. At other times it reflects positive parts of ourselves that we have not yet developed. It is the side of ourselves that we aren't paying attention to, and it is also where much of our untapped potential power for change resides. One of life's great ironies is that, the more you can accept what is true right now, the more you are able to change it. As you embark on the Circle of Life process, you will discover that being honest about what is happening—or not happening—right now, will become your best ally in making your life work better than ever before.

The Circle of Life process has six small steps. First you will draw a circle, and then you will divide the circle into slices, naming each slice with the important areas of your life. Next you will notice how you are doing with each area, giving each slice a grade indicating how you feel this area is working. For example, if you feel good about your exercise program, you would give exercise a grade of "good." Other areas of your life might feel "okay," and finally others will feel they "need some improvement." Then you will learn how to score and rate the items in your circle. Next you will consider the goals you have, or the small action steps you are willing to take to improve some areas. Finally, in step six you will visualize and imagine your life just as you would like it to be. We will go over each of these steps in complete detail.

Your Dreams

As you go through this book, you will see questions that are designed to help you focus your attention on specific areas of your life, such as relationships, health, happiness, career, spirituality, finances, goals, dreams, and aspirations. The questions are designed to help you evaluate your life in objective terms. You will choose the areas that are most relevant to your personal path. Whether this is a private process that nobody else sees, or you want to share it with a significant other or paste it on your vision board for the world to see, is entirely up to you.

As you begin to make your circle, answer the questions in terms of what is happening right now, not how it used to be or how you would like it to be. The answers should reflect a snapshot of how things are in this moment. By being truthful in your responses, you reclaim control over your world. The more truthful you are, the more you will benefit from this process.

Sometimes people come into therapy thinking that one area or another of their life isn't working. When they do the Circle of Life process, they see the interconnections, and they often have an entirely new perspective when they look at their life as a whole. When you complete your personal Circle of Life, you can see your entire life at a glance. This is often surprisingly exciting—because it also shows you what is working. Most of us are used to focusing on certain areas of life, often the ones we think *aren't* working. Perhaps you've been ignoring or not paying sufficient attention to areas in which you are doing fairly well. Many of my patients experience a boost of optimism when they realize that it is just a few areas of their lives that need work. And they also realize that they may have taken for granted other areas that just seem to be going well and are flowing naturally.

> ### The Six Steps of the Circle of Life
>
> 1. Draw your Circle and Divide it into Slices
>
> 2. Fill in the Slices with the Important Areas of Your Life
>
> 3. Give Each Slice a Grade—"Good," or "Okay," or "Needs Improvement"
>
> 4. Score the Total Grades to Get a Snapshot of Your Life Right Now
>
> 5. List or Write Out Your Personal Goals and the Small Action Steps You Are Willing to Take
>
> 6. Use Your Imagination and Visualize with Intention to Draw You to the Perfect Life of Your Dreams.

It is always a fun moment when my patients hold their completed Circle of Life in their hands and see their life as a whole. Patterns they hadn't noticed become clear, and significant insights often follow. Seeing your whole life on a page helps you to see areas that you wish to change, as well as areas that are working nicely. You may even feel a deep rush of gratitude for those areas where you have a certain sense of mastery.

Once you are ready to start filling in your circle, the process takes around a half-hour to an hour to complete. You can choose what areas are relevant and important for you to focus on. Sometimes we feel unhappy with our life—but we can't quite pinpoint why. This process will help you identify previously unknown reasons and imbalances that cause that nagging dissatisfaction. You will also see how one area of your life impacts another. The resulting clarity shifts the balance of your self-perception and is very empowering.

After you have created your unique Circle of Life, the next move is to decide to take one or two small, specific steps that take you more in the direction of your heart's desires. This is a gentle and easy process. It's your life, and no one can tell you what to change. When you see it all together, you can take a step back and get new perspectives on where you want to go. You will decide what you want to change, and what you are willing to change, and how soon you want to get started. Then, as things improve, you will be even more motivated to make the next small—or perhaps large—change. It begins to inspire you when you see that change is not so hard when you don't have to change every area at once. It is exciting to see that, when you make the right small changes, they can have a huge positive impact on several areas of your life, as you will read later in Alex's story.

As a therapist, I value this process, because instead of just "telling" my patients what or how to change, with the Circle of Life process I put the tools of change back into their hands. They can now begin to make their own best choices and decisions. I make suggestions, of course, as I assist them to uncover their own creativity and enthusiasm for change. I encourage patients to begin by identifying one or two areas they really want to change, and make only the small, concrete changes they feel truly excited about doing. Building and strengthening small action steps is what ultimately leads to larger changes. It is delightful to watch people embrace their lives and begin to make some small decisions and changes that have a major and direct impact on their life. With no one telling you what to do or not to do, you are always in control of the pace and scope of change.

For people who are in relationships, the Circle of Life really opens their awareness of what is working and what is not—which can take the pressure off believing the problem is with the other person. When you can begin to see your own true needs, you can set better boundaries and make better choices.

The Circle of Life process encourages you to make changes—and you have a high probability of success, because you are making only the changes you are ready and willing to make. As one small area begins to improve, you focus on the next, and in this way you fine-tune your process and continually build on the new growth. This begins a positive spiral, where you have a method and a plan for lifelong adjustment moving you towards everything you truly want. It allows you to let go of "false goals," which are goals that don't really ring true for you. There is no right or wrong to the process at any step of the way. This means you can't get it wrong.

Your personal Circle of Life is not a fixed map. It is always changing, and it can be a truly wonderful ritual to update or do a new Circle of Life at significant points in your life cycle, such as your birthday, New Year's Day, anniversaries, when making life changes, or whatever timeframe is meaningful to you. In this way, it reminds you that you are a work in progress. This will help you feel engaged and encouraged in the process of designing your future life.

Your Circle of Life is your ever-changing, living, evolving map to everything you want in life. Here's the story of Alex and how the Circle of Life process helped him to identify that he needed to make some changes in the area of health habits. These changes ultimately led him to make some other big changes in his life.

Alex's Story

Alex, age 42, was a graphic artist who was partners with two friends in a start-up web-design company. Due to the need to keep expenses down, and because he was the best of the three at technical skills, he ended up being the one in the company doing the programming and technical aspects, and was spending less and less time on the creative elements that had motivated him to join forces with his friends in the first place. Although, on the surface, he understood the need for this focus, he was underestimating the toll it was taking on his life.

When Alex came into therapy, his complaints were depression and problems focusing. He had been gaining weight that year, had no time for a real relationship, and had lost interest in dating. When we began working on his Circle of Life, I asked him if sleep was an issue. He thought for a moment and said, "Not really." As we went through the questions, it became clear that he was getting only about five hours of sleep a night. His bedroom was filled with electronic devices, such as his 40-inch plasma TV, a laptop and desktop computer, two cell phone chargers on his nightstand, two alarm clocks with LED lights. In short, he was sleeping in a cocoon of electromagnetic frequencies. The room was never completely dark, because of the glow of screens, which was likely affecting the quality of his sleep.

His bedspread was something his ex-wife had bought. It had a loud pattern, in colors he never really liked. He still had the same pillow he had used in college. His double bed seemed always to have technical manuals on it.

Within five minutes, it became clear that the symptoms he was describing—trouble concentrating, not thinking clearly for the necessarily long periods of time he needed to do his work well, decreasing enthusiasm about his social life, and easy irritability—were all possibly related to the lack of quantity and quality of sleep.

He didn't believe this was a problem at first, but he was intrigued enough to experiment. He decided to be diligent about getting seven to eight hours of sleep. He stopped watching the news before bed, and took the computers out of his bedroom.

He shopped online for a new "bed in a bag" in a solid color of blue that really appealed to him, and even got a new memory foam pillow, which helped with the dull pain he was having in his neck. Since he wasn't watching intense TV news before turning in, he was going to bed in a calmer state.

The first night in his "new room" he went to sleep by eleven and for the first time in months slept straight through the night for seven hours. Without all the electronics, his brain was not being artificially pulled into alert rapid brain wave frequencies, and he was able to naturally fall into the deeper theta and delta sleep zones. He woke up feeling renewed and energized, and has been sleeping better ever since.

This one change improved his energy, concentration, and state of mind. He felt more positive about his partners and his future. They began having more productive conversations about the future of the company, and communication levels were more satisfying. With his improved mood, he was more attractive to everyone around him, and the girl in the office down the hall finally asked him out for coffee. Unlike his usual pattern of rushing, he felt calm enough to take his time. They've had several dates, and he is feeling optimistic about having a deeper relationship with her.

Although Alex didn't realize that sleep was such an issue, this is an example of how change in one important area of his life led to significant positive changes that gave him the energy and willingness he needed to take on some further changes with his partners and his business. He was really inspired by how easy it is to improve your life when you make the *right* changes.

CHAPTER 2

What Your Circle of Life Tells You about Your Life

Beginning to create your circle can be as simple or as ornate as you choose. You can just use a piece of plain paper. Or you can use a beautiful journal or artist's sketch pad or any notebook for your Circle of Life process. The wonderful thing about having a special book is that you can keep all of your Circles of Life together. As you make new circles each year, you can look back from time to time to notice all the progress you've made.

When I am working with patients in my office, I use a large flip chart to make the circle. I use colored markers. Having a big visual image allows us both to interact and dialogue about the items on the circle and to discuss these issues over time.

You'll find you can be very creative with your Circle of Life. You can use colored pens or pencils for the different slices, descriptions, or new goals. Let the Circle of Life process open your mind to your own creative flow and discover the mandala (which is a circular visual expression or picture) of your own life.

Or, if gathering these items creates obstacles to getting started, just grab a piece of white paper from your computer printer and a pen or pencil, and you have everything you need. You can always transfer your circle to a more permanent book later. Or make a special file folder where you can keep track of your Circles of Life, to watch how your life unfolds over the years. Some people like to do this process in a leather-bound book. I have teens who write on a piece of loose-leaf paper. Don't let anything get in the way of beginning. Whatever method feels good to you is the right method for you.

Some people like to do this process with a friend or partner. Others feel this is a very private process and want to do it on their own. Sometimes they may choose to share it with a significant other at a later date. Whatever inspires you to do your Circle of Life will be perfect.

Let's take a little look ahead at areas of focus, or slices, as I call them, so you can see what areas of your life will be represented in your Circle of Life process. You will see all the important areas—everything from sleep, diet, exercise, to mental health, hobbies and relaxation, to relationships, goals, dreams and aspirations . . . and you can add your own areas of interest and importance to you. You will also see some questions that will help you get started creating your own personal Circle of Life.

Here are some suggested slices for your Circle of Life

Sleep

Diet

Exercise

Relaxation / Stress Management

Physical Health

Mental Health / Self-Esteem

Hobbies

Friends / Co-Workers

Family

Significant Other

Children

Spirituality

Goals / Dreams / Aspirations

Income / Finances

Work / Job / Career

School / Education/ Training

Pets (if you don't have any, you can skip this slice)

Home Environment / Personal Space

Personal Areas of Interest: Sexuality, Intimacy, Body Image, Communication

Optional Areas: Communication, Fun, Adventure, Entertainment, Travel, etc.

Getting Started With Your Circle of Life

The first step to changing your life begins with giving yourself a gift of about a half-hour or more of uninterrupted time to create your personal Circle of Life. Are you ready to own your life? Good. Then make this your private time; it's all yours; don't let anything interfere, because you deserve this!

Let's begin by bringing all your awareness to this moment by focusing on the present. After you read this, you might want to take a couple of moments to close your eyes and follow your breath, allowing your breathing to slow down your thoughts. This is not a time to worry about the future, or replay regrets about the past. This is all about putting your entire focus on the present.

Make a promise to yourself to be totally truthful as you do this process. No one has to see this, so just tell the truth because it is the truth that will set you free to enjoy this process.

Begin by drawing a large circle that fills up about ¾ of your page size. Use a compass, or round plate or anything convenient to help you draw your circle. Put today's date with the year at the top corner of the page.

In Chapter Three you will find detailed information on how the suggested slices represent the various and important areas of your life. Think of them as slices of the "pie" of your life. If some slices don't fit or you need to add others, go ahead. Some areas may not be relevant (such as if you don't have children and aren't looking to have them, or if you don't have any pets). School may not be relevant, so you may replace that category with something else that is personally important to you. For example, if there is an area such as communication that is very important to you, go ahead and add that. Make sure to include all the slices that apply, even if you don't think they are active parts of your life. Even if you can't think of how you will fill them, just put them in your circle for now.

Choose the areas you want to include. In general, most adults seem to have between 15 and 18 slices in order to represent a full life experience. Count the total and divide your circle into that number of slices. For example, if you have chosen 18 areas, you will divide your "pie" into eighteen slices. Write the names of the slices in each slot. You might choose to have all the slice-names in one color, and the descriptions in another color. It all depends on what appeals to your eye and what inspires you.

Add Your Unique Slices

If you have a particular area of interest other than the 18 slices suggested, feel free to add them now. This might be an area of your life that is meaningful to you—or it could be a problem area that you want to focus on. Or it could be something that is missing that you would really like to have in your life. Add a slice for anything that would be important. Examples might be adding slices for travel, getting an education or training, sexuality, intimacy, partnership or communication, or more creativity.

If it is something you want included in your life—even if it doesn't exist right now—add it in. Later you will learn how to take steps to bring this slice into your reality. By making a slice for this area, you begin to make it real. Having its own slice helps to evolve this area and gather energy and focus.

One of my patients had a life goal of climbing Mount Everest. To prepare for her climb, she created a slice for this goal. This helped her organize her thinking and prepare for all the steps for the journey the following summer.

Review the questions in the next chapter for each area or

Circle of Life

Name _____

Date _____

- Mental Health Self Esteem
- Physical Health
- Relaxation Stress Management
- Hobbies
- Exercise
- Friends Co-workers
- Diet
- Family Origin
- Sleep
- Significant Other
- Home
- Children
- Pets
- Spirituality
- Education/Training
- Goals, Dreams, Aspirations
- Finances
- Career/Job

+	Good
✔	Okay
–	Needs Improvement

slice. These questions are designed to trigger your own creative ideas. You may have other questions that are even more important to you personally. Then make notes, either on a separate worksheet or on one of the blank pages included in this book.

Then transfer short summary phrases that pertain to each slice right onto your circle. For example, for sleep you might write "sleep 7 hours," or "waking up" and "hard to get back to sleep." For diet you might write "eating too much ice cream." For exercise you might write "jogging three times a week." For hobbies you might write "ballroom dancing." In other words, this is not about creating a list of things you might consider "good" or "bad." This is a visual description of exactly what is going on in your life right in this moment.

Be gentle with yourself. This is not an inquisition—just be honest. Remember this is not about writing what it used to be like, or what you wish it would be like, but just how it truthfully is in this moment, today!

For some slices you may have a lot to say, others not as much. Just pick the most pertinent slices for your life and fill out each as best you can. For example, if you have no hobbies at all, you can write "no hobbies." Having this note may help you later as we work on the next layers of the Circle of Life.

Continue this process until you have filled in your whole Circle of Life. It is great to do this in one sitting, because the idea is to write your first gut responses to the slices.

Now take a moment to step back and look at what you have created. Acknowledge what you have done. Be sure to notice the areas that are functioning well. This process encourages you to focus on the positives as well as areas that you want to improve. Focusing for some moments on the positive builds your enthusiasm for your own ability to change, and raises your willingness to consider making more changes. It will also really serve you to feel some gratitude for the parts of your life that are working well.

In Chapter Four I will show you how to score your circle, meaning that you will give each slice a possible rating of "good," "okay," or "needs improvement," based on your opinion of how you feel you are doing in each area.

In Chapter Five I will show you how to take the next step with your circle, which is creating the outer ring. This outer ring is a picture of what you want to create in your life. It is a listing of the small steps you plan to take in order to create the changes you want to see. This is where you want to focus your energy. This outer ring is truly the circle of transformation that will bring your life to the next level.

CHAPTER 3

Creating the Slices of Your Circle of Life

Here is a reminder of the suggested slices that you may want to include in your Circle of Life. Eliminate any that aren't relevant to your personal situation, and add any others that have importance in your life.

The Slices for Your Circle of Life:

Sleep

Diet

Exercise

Relaxation / Stress Management

Physical Health

Mental Health / Self-Esteem

Hobbies

Friends / Co-Workers

Family

Significant Other

Children

Spirituality

Goals / Dreams / Aspirations

Income / Finances

Work / Job / Career

School / Education / Training

Pets (If you don't have any, you can skip this slice)

Home Environment / Personal Space

Personal Areas of Focus: Sexuality / Intimacy / Body Image / Communication

Optional Areas: Fun, Adventure, Entertainment, Travel, etc.

These are suggested areas. You may not need all of these, or you may have personal ones that you wish to add. For example, as I said before, if you have no children or pets, you might substitute some other area that is important to you. What follows is a brief discussion of each area to spark your thinking process.

Sleep

Sleep is the basis of mental and physical health. Having a regular sleep pattern will promote an optimal life. Yet many people are not getting the sleep they need to function at their best. It would be a good first step to look at this important area of your life and see how you are doing. Below are some questions to inspire your thinking. They may not all be relevant to your situation, but they are designed to raise your awareness of how sleep is functioning in your life.

This chapter provides a list of questions that you may ask yourself in order to stimulate important information to add in your Circle of Life. Answering these questions will help you determine what is important to list in your slices. Add your own relevant questions to keep you focused on what's important.

Here are some suggested questions to help you with your Sleep Slice:

- How many hours do I need? How many hours am I getting?
- Do I like my mattress, pillows, blankets, sheets, and bedspread?
- How is the temperature/air flow in the room?
- How is the lighting in the room? Do I like to sleep in darkness? Or do I need some light on in the room?
- Do I like the direction of my bed? Does it feel right to me?
- Is there too much or too little furniture?

Do I like the colors in the room or on the bed? Carpet? Curtains? Wall decorations?

Is it quiet or noisy? Do I play music to go to sleep? Do I watch TV?

Do I have my cell phone, computer, TV, clock, LEDs near my bed?

Is there clutter? Or is my bedroom well organized and visually peaceful?

Do I have trouble falling asleep / staying asleep?

Do I wake up refreshed?

Do I use an alarm clock? Is it pleasant or unpleasant?

Am I getting up in the night—for the bathroom? Is it difficult to get back to sleep? Do I wake up feeling refreshed or tired?

Do I take any sleep medications or natural supplements?

Is my or my partner's snoring an issue?

Do I or my partner have issues with sleep apnea?

Do I dream? Are my dreams in color, or black and white?

Do I have nightmares? Are there recurrent themes?

Do I use sound, ear plugs, or a sleep mask to insure sound sleep?

Diet

It is said that you are what you eat. What you put in your body shows up as your body's energy. If you are not putting the right fuel in, you can't expect your body to perform at optimal levels. If your body is constantly fighting toxins or unknown food allergies, this can have a huge impact on your mood, your ability to concentrate, and general energy levels.

- Do I eat breakfast? What do I eat? Where do I eat?
- Do I snack? What time of day do I reach for snacks? What kind?
- Do I eat lunch? What do I eat? Healthy or unhealthy?
- Do I eat dinner? What time? Do I eat alone or with others?
- Am I on a diet?
- Do I know what foods are best for me?
- How often do I eat? How often do I eat fast or processed food?
- Do I drink enough water?
- Do I take vitamins and/or supplements?
- How much do I eat?
- Are there any foods that I overeat? What are they?
- Which meals do I often miss?
- Do I have any eating problems that can cause health issues such as bulimia and anorexia?
- Do I feel energized after I eat?
- Do I have any digestive issues?
- Am I an "emotional eater" . . . stuffing food, or starving, when I feel emotional about people or situations in my life?

Exercise

Exercise is essential for the quality of life. Not only does it keep the body active, but your brain, your heart, your lungs, and your hormone production all work better when you exercise. Keeping the body active is one of the best things you can do to promote well-being. What type of exercise you choose doesn't matter that much; however, doing it consistently will make a huge difference in your physical and mental health.

- Am I exercising? How often?
- Do I enjoy my exercise?
- Is my exercise primarily a solo activity? Or done with others?
- Do I exercise for health? For fun? For sport? As a hobby?
- Do I get a variety of exercise opportunities?
- What kind of exercise am I doing? Walking, running, dancing, weight lifting, going to the gym, martial arts, hiking, biking, swimming, surfing, sports, cardio, strength training, cross training, skiing, etc.
- Do I exercise to full or partial capacity?
- Do I want to do more exercise? Or less exercise?

Relaxation

Relaxation is a very important balance to all the busyness in life. Relaxation brings us back to our human "being-ness." It allows us to let go of stress. It also helps us get in touch with our true feelings and desires. When we get too busy with outside activities, it can cause us to forget our own needs. Relaxation can be a very important tool to help you reconnect with your inner self.

Relaxation can be a formal or ritual process that you do on a regular basis, or it can be any simple activity (or non-activity, such as just lying in a hammock!) that allows you to reconnect with yourself in the moment.

Some examples of relaxation might be: massage, meditation, listening to music, deep breathing, taking a pleasurable bath, napping, enjoying the beach, being in nature, or visiting favorite places.

Stress Management

- How do I manage or cope with my stress?
- What are the causes of stress in my life?
- What do I do when I feel stress?
- Do I feel like I'm managing my stress effectively?
- When do I feel stress?
- Why are the stressors in my life?
- Where in my body do I hold onto stress?
- What kind of thoughts do I have when I am stressed?
- What self-destructive actions do I take when under stress?
- Are there some better choices I could make when I feel stress?

Physical Health

Without health, you don't have the energy to help or improve any other area of your life, so health is the most important aspect of your life. When you are in good health, you can easily accomplish your dreams, goals, and aspirations. When your health is challenged, it is hard to focus on relationships, career, or any other forward moving area of your life.

Look at your total health—from inside and outside your body—to see what health issues you might have. Answer the following questions. Your answers will give you a good assessment of your total health.

- How is my health? What are my health concerns?
- Do I get regular medical and dental check-ups?
- Do I have health insurance?
- Am I on over-the-counter or prescription medications?
- Do I take herbal or natural supplements and vitamins?
- Do I visit natural or alternative health practitioners?
- How do I feel about my weight?
- Is health a priority in my life?
- What steps am I taking to promote my health?
- What areas of health do I feel need more attention?
- Are there some medical tests I feel I need to take?
- What are the areas that are healthy and working well?

As you focus on the *inside* of your body you might notice if any of these areas are issues: allergies, asthma, heart problems, cholesterol, circulation, headaches, breathing, libido, digestive problems, stiff joints, aches and pains, etc.

As you focus on the *outside* of your body are there any issues with: skin, hands, wrists, fingers, arms, shoulders, neck, chest, back, hips, legs, knees, feet, toes, ears, eyes, nose, mouth, teeth, hair, etc.

Mental Health / Self Esteem

In this slice you are exploring cognitive and emotional issues that express how you think and feel. How you are doing in this area of your life makes a difference in every decision you make. Everything you do in the world, and the way you "show up" to other people, begins with your own sense of self.

Self-Esteem—

- How do I feel about myself?
- What are those feelings most of the time?
- How do I feel about my body?
    - What is my level of self-acceptance?
- Self-Concept—What do I think about myself?
    - What is my self-talk? Is it generally positive or negative?
    - How is my self-confidence?
- What feelings do I feel most often?
    - Anxiety, fear, sadness, anger, resentment, disappointment, depression, frustration, loneliness?
- How often do I feel these feelings: happy, joyful, peaceful, enthusiastic, courageous, inspired, and optimistic?

- Do I have a support group, caring friends, or compassionate family members?

Hobbies

Hobbies are important for a balanced life. A hobby can be any activity that brings you pleasure, fulfillment, or satisfaction. The "right" hobby for you is a very personal choice, and what brings you pleasure may be unique. Some people can readily point to their hobbies and are already spending time pursuing them. For other people, this area of life is a total blank. Having a hobby is important, because it means you are balancing the other demands of life and taking time for yourself, which brings you a greater feeling of control and self-satisfaction.

Maybe you had hobbies as a child; maybe you never did. If not, consider this a wonderful area to explore. Having a good hobby or two can greatly add to the feeling of quality in your life.

Here are some hobbies my clients have discovered: singing, cooking, reading, art, crafts, painting, volunteering, collecting, sewing, photography, videography, computer games, journaling, cars, bikes, culture, arts, music, films, theater, poetry, gardening, dancing, repairing, rebuilding, feng shui, to name a few.

Some people will put their desires for travel in this section. For others, travel is such an important goal that it deserves its own slice.

Friends / Co-Workers

The importance of social connections—through friends, support groups, acquaintances, church groups—cannot be overstated. Connections with others are essential to mental and physical health. Even if you are in a relationship, having friendships plays a very important role in hormone production and balance. For women, good conversations with other women increase oxytocin (the "love chemical"). For men, interacting with other men increases testosterone.

It is helpful to have a range of friends. Some may be close, while others may just be people you chat with now and then. They are all important to your happiness and sense of connection. Good friends are people you feel close to, people whom you can trust in order to share deeply about yourself. Acquaintances are people you know, but they don't know that much about you at a deeper level. It's not unusual for many people to have friends from work since we spend so many hours working.

Take a look at the friends in your life (or notice if you feel this slice is fairly empty). This will give you a good, objective view of how connected you are to others. It is not the number of friends, but the quality of the connection and intimacy you feel with them. This is an important slice about which to be honest with yourself.

Friends

- Do I have best or close friends? Who are the people with whom I do fun things or spend time?
- How often do I see my good friends?

- How much time do I spend with good friends?
- How often am I in touch with old friends?
- Do I have acquaintances—from work, school, church, neighborhood, community?

Family

Your family provides your roots. It forms the basis of who you are. Your family gives you the first contact with other people; they are your first teachers during your formative years. These relationships are important for your life, whether you are close or not. This is the reason why we want to look at the nature of your relationship with each of your family members.

Who are the members of your family? List them.

- How are your relationships with each of these members?
- Overall, how do you feel about your relationships with your family?
- Are you part of a blended or step-family?
- Are you adopted?
- Did your parents come from different cultures?
- Did you grow up in a multi-cultural home?

Significant Other

This section explores your closest personal relationship. With your significant other you have the opportunity to develop skills on a deeper level. You can share and create a life with a companion or lover.

Sometimes circumstances will cause you to be separated from your significant other, but you still have a relationship with that person. If you are divorced, you may be sharing parenting. Perhaps this relationship is in a state of transformation—is it difficult, or has it translated into friendship?

What is the quality of this relationship?

- What problems and challenges are you having?
- Is there intimacy?
- How is the communication?
- Do you want to have a significant other?
- Are you recovering from a relationship?
  Do you have trust issues?
- Are you ready to get involved?
- Are you dating? Do you want to date?
  Do you know how to date?
- Are you open? Looking? Receptive?
- Are you preparing for one?
- Are you praying for one?

Children

If you don't have or don't want children, you can skip this slice. If children are part of your present or your future, spend some time with this slice. Ask yourself:

- Are there children in your life? How many? What ages?
- Are they yours or your significant other's?
- Do you have step-children? Or adopted or foster children?
- Are the children enhancing your life, or causing you stress?
- What are your relationships with them like?
- Do you have any issues with them?
- Do you have parenting issues?
- Is your life child-centered or adult-centered?

Spirituality

This area explores your personal relationship to the universe or your religious beliefs.

- What is your personal or spiritual relationship to the universe?
- Do you have a spiritual practice?
- Is religion a part of your life?
- Do you attend a church, temple, mosque, or other place of worship?
- Beliefs: What are your guiding principles?
    - Do you believe there is a God or a Higher Power, or an Infinite Intelligence?
    - Do you believe in karma ("What goes

around comes around")? Or cause and effect? Do you believe in reincarnation?

- Do you believe in or practice The Golden Rule ("Do unto others as you would have them do unto you")?
- What are your key beliefs about life, the universe, and human nature?

Goals / Dreams / Aspirations

In this section you look at your heart's desires: your goals, dreams, and aspirations. *Goals* are concrete, with a measurable destination—in the sense that you know when you complete the process and have accomplished your goal. These are specific "do-able" things that you intend to accomplish, or things that you want to own or have.

Dreams are your heart's desires. They are things you would like to have in your life. These are your sometimes private imaginings.

Aspirations are your cherished desires. They are what you are reaching for and moving toward in your life right now. Your ambitions and grand desires are your aspirations. For example, you might be aspiring to be a writer, or mother, or doctor, etc. Your aspirations are a process. They are your journey of life.

- Goals: What are your goals in life?
- Dreams: What do you imagine for yourself and your life? What are your dreams?
- Aspirations: What are you reaching for?

Income / Finances

How are you doing with the money in your life? Are you earning it (or not)? How are you handling money?
Finances: How are you doing with . . . ?

- Salary & income?
- Savings?
- Checking?
- Investments?
- Retirement?
- Paying off debts?

Work / Job / Career

There are differences among these three categories. A job is something you do to earn money. A career offers professional advancement. A calling is a job or profession that you are passionate about. When you look at this area of your life, do you feel you are on purpose or in alignment with your personal life goals?

- Do you feel that you are on purpose or in alignment with your greater goals?
- If you are interested in advancement, do you have opportunities?
- Are you earning a good living?
- How do you feel about your boss or co-workers?

- How would you rate your level of satisfaction?
- Do you like the environment where you work?
- Do you want to stay with this job?
- What changes do you want to make?

Education / School / Training

Are you in school, involved in continued learning, or in special training, academic or vocational? Do you have further educational goals that you would like to pursue?

- How do you feel about your educational process?
- How well are you doing?
- How much further do you have to go?
- When will you complete your school or training?
- What are your expectations for completing this program?
- What are your educational plans?
- Are you dealing with student loans? Or do you need to apply for one?

Pets

If you don't have pets, or don't wish to have them in the future, you can skip this slice.

Having animals can make you feel like they are part of your family. They can greatly add to the sense of love and meaning in your life. Do these animals live in the same space as you live, sleep, and eat? Do they live in the yard or farther away? Some pets are like best friends or family; others are like acquaintances. What kind of pets do you have? Dogs, cats, birds, fish—something more exotic? They can all add to the quality of your life.

- Which pets do you have? What are their names?
- Are you mourning over the loss of pets?
- Do you have any issues with pets?
- What positive qualities do they bring into your life?
- Are there any conflicts with others regarding your pets?

Home Environment / Personal Space

This is where you spend your personal time. Home is a very personal space. It is a very important area of your life in terms of understanding what is happening in your emotional or physical space. Ideally, your home space provides you with a sense of peace and comfort. Hopefully it is conducive to your lifestyle and is comfortable for both your basic and pleasure-based needs. You may have a private personal space, or you may be sharing it with others. How your home environment is working for you has a great impact on the quality of your life.

- How do I feel about my home environment?
- How do I feel about the location of my home environment?

- Does it provide peace/comfort/safety?
- What is the level of organization vs. clutter?
- Is this a shared space with others?
- Do I have private or alone space or areas?
- Do I feel in control or out of control of my space? In what ways?
- Is there privacy?
- Is it quiet or noisy?
- Does it reflect my taste in furnishings?
- Do I truly feel safe and protected?
- Have I been at risk for homelessness?

Add Your Own Personal Slices

You may have some areas of your life that are important and personal to you. Feel free to add in any of these areas as slices in your Circle of Life. Here are some personal areas you may want to focus on: intimacy and communication, dating, sexuality, weight control, or any others that are relevant to your life and desires.

If, for example, you have a desire to travel and this is important to you and to the design of your life, add travel as its own slice. Travel can be a wonderful way to expand your experience or vistas, and get out of your routine and change perspective. If you have a desire to see new people, places, or things, create a travel slice and include where you would like to travel and other details and plans for your travel desires.

- Do you want to travel?
- Do you have any travel plans?
- What is your purpose/desire for travel? Pleasure? Work? Hobby? Culture? Opportunities? Curiosity? Education? Family roots? Adventure?

Enjoy this process and add any slices that will make your Circle of Life the perfect expression of your desires. This will help you to remember that change is a process, not a destination. The journey begins by putting it all down on paper and moving one step forward every day.

CHAPTER

4

How to Transform Your Life

Scoring Your Circle

Now that you have created the first three steps of your Circle of Life, you move on to Step Four, which is scoring your circle. Contemplate each slice, and intuitively decide to give each of them one of the following three possible scores. You can rate a slice as "Good," meaning that, overall, you're doing *well* in this area. "Okay" means you're doing *all right* in this area. Or, finally, you might feel that a particular slice "Needs Improvement." Don't spend a long time thinking; just quickly, off the top of your head, assign the score that feels most accurate to you in this moment.

If your score is GOOD, put a PLUS sign on the outer rim of that slice.

If your score is OKAY, put a CHECK sign on the outer rim of that slice.

If your score is NEEDS IMPROVEMENT, put a MINUS sign on the outer rim of that slice.

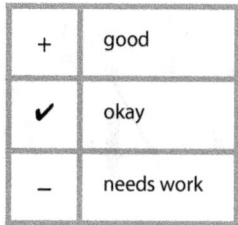

Don't fret or obsess about what score to give; just trust your first instinct. You intuitively know what is and isn't working in your life. You may be surprised how easy it is to score these slices. Remember to be completely honest, as this is *your* Circle of Life. The more accurate your score is, the more useful it will be for you, because you can see how much you have changed when you look back at your circle some time later. Also, the more truthful you are, the more you will have precise guidance on how to make transformative decisions in the future.

Now . . . create a small table of three columns at the bottom of the page of your Circle of Life, as in the example shown. List your *pluses* at the top, then below, your *checks*, and then your *minuses*.

Adding Your Scores:

Add up your scores (see table). How many pluses, checks, and minuses do you have in your life?

For example, you might end up with a score of 8 "Goods," 6 "Okays," 4 "Needs Improvement," or any combination.

As you look at your completed Circle of Life, just observe this map of your life. Like a satellite shot from outer space, it is an overview of the essence of how things are for you in this moment. Having a realistic assessment is what allows you to focus on simple and specific action steps that can give your life the proper momentum—not just expenditure of energy. The perspective of this broad view gives you valuable feedback. Unless you understand where you are, you won't know where you want to go, or how to get there.

Now that you have assessed your life score, ask yourself: "Do I feel that the number of pluses, checks, and minuses accurately describes my life today?" It's amazing how often the answer is "yes." At this point I frequently hear how wonderful the process has been. As you can see your entire life depicted in a circle, the opportunity presents itself to make life a conscious process. You can see where your life is right now, how you feel about it, and how you can get in touch with your desires, motivations, and enthusiasm to make changes and move in the direction you want to go.

What do you notice as you look at your circle? As you look at the scores and see what areas they are in, do you see patterns emerging? One of my patients, Sherry, did this. She realized that, because she had been so busy with her kids, her time with them had all pluses, but it had taken over her life and she wasn't spending any time on herself. The areas that needed improvement in her life were the personal time areas such as sleep, exercise, relaxation, hobbies, mental health, and spirituality. She couldn't even imagine how it would be to spend time by herself. As soon as she understood this, she began a simple action plan. She started exercising, and walking the dog with her husband in the evening. They made Saturday a date night together. Within ninety days of making small changes, she felt like a different person.

Sometimes people look at the large issues in their lives and think they need to make huge changes in order to get the results they want. While sometimes a crisis can provide both an opportunity and a demand for sudden and dramatic change, for the most part effective change occurs through small but consistent steps in the right direction. Many small changes lead to big changes that are stable enough to be sustained.

Even the tiniest change is beneficial. The advantage of committing to taking tiny steps is that the mind doesn't resist them as much as an enormous change in behavior would be threatening. Small steps don't cause as much emotional backlash. Like the fable, it is better to be like the tortoise, slow and steady, than to burst ahead like the hare and then find that you have exhausted yourself and give up. It is like going back to the gym: you don't want to overdo it on your first visit, injure yourself, and then quit.

Another benefit of making consistent small changes is that what the brain focuses on, you get more of. The brain prioritizes what you are emphasizing most. Placing your attention on positive changes can lead to more willingness to move in that direction. A big change can cause you to resist because it feels so far outside your comfort zone. It is not necessary, however, to leap out of your comfort zone. Ridiculously small steps can lead to great success.

Some examples of small changes patients made were:

- Going to bed fifteen minutes earlier.
- Parking at the farthest point in the parking lot to get two five-minute walks in a day.
- Drinking one more glass of water a day.
- Stretching for two minutes in the shower.
- Writing one item in a journal to be grateful for each day.
- Calling one's mother or father once a week.
- Eating only half a portion of dessert.

All of these tiny changes produced great results and a sense of empowerment that led to making more positive and bigger changes.

Of course, big innovative changes can be wonderful. If you feel that making a big leap would give you more momentum and power, by all means go for it. For some people, it is easier to make the huge plunge than to take small steps. Here is where you need to know yourself and know what works best for you. Choose the size of the change that will work for you in this moment. By choosing the size and scope of the change you think will give you the best results, you are more likely to succeed and you will have the least resistance.

Raising Your Score

So as you look at your completed Circle of Life, ask yourself, "What simple action steps would I be willing to take to raise any of my scores?" What is one concrete thing that you are really motivated to do, that would turn a minus into a check, or a check into a plus? Even taking one small action-step can affect your happiness and raise your score. It is often very exciting to see how one small change improves your mood, inspiring you to make other changes you weren't even thinking about. They just begin to unfold naturally, because you are in a more positive frame of mind. I see this over and over, and when you read the case studies you will see how many times getting one area working has a large and sometimes global impact on other areas.

I am emphasizing this "brick-by-brick" layering process of small changes leading to larger ones, because you get to see immediate results as the quality of your life is enhanced. The secret is not to try to change everything overnight. Rather, let one change work like the domino effect, influencing other areas in a positive manner. Look for changes that feel simple, natural, and authentic. Like the journey of a thousand miles, it starts with the first step.

The next step is to write some new goals right on the outside of each slice. This is the outer circle where you write your "Action Steps." These are the simple, specific activities that you would be willing to do that will help you make the larger changes you want. The key here is to keep it simple and do-able.

This outer circle of transformation is where you direct towards a future of achieving your goals and dreams. You will manifest whatever changes you place your intention on by focusing on an action step you are genuinely willing to achieve, you will be successful. Your mind will prioritize the goal for you and support your decision.

Here is an example. Sara, a single mom, had been wondering about going back to school. Feeling overwhelmed by the whole idea, she hadn't taken a step towards this goal that had been rambling around in her brain for eight years. She came up with her first action step: "Identify three schools that look appealing." In other words, she reduced the entire issue of "Should I go back to school?"—A huge issue that felt insurmountable to her—to its most basic "do-able" step, which was identifying three schools that seemed a good educational fit and offered her online classes in her areas of interest. In just a week of online research, she had identified the three most suitable schools, whereupon she immediately took the next action step, which was ordering their catalogues.

Although Sara had two different majors—she was considering both psychology and education (an unresolved quandary that had kept her from taking any action!)—the trick was not to worry about answering that larger question yet. Her goal was to read each catalogue's description in her two areas of interest. Then she gave herself thirty days to decide which school to apply to. In this simple way, her ten-year procrastination easily came to an end.

In other words, she reduced her big issue down to the smallest action steps. In Sara's case, she needed to allow the larger question to remain "unanswered," but still to take a simple action that led her in the right direction. Even if she wasn't sure in which area she wanted the degree, she could begin to act, which led to getting more information (actual school catalogues that described her two programs) so that she could come to greater clarity. Thirty days later, she felt clear enough to apply to one of the schools. By breaking larger actions into the smallest do-able steps, she could see that progress is possible and change is manageable.

As you are looking to identify your action steps, the question is: "Is it do-able?" Ask yourself: "Will this action make a difference or point me in the right direction of my goal?" These may be steps that have been in the back of your mind for a while, or you may have an entirely new inspiration as you ask these questions. The trick is not to become overwhelmed by this part of the process. Using the example of going back to school, don't worry about how to apply for financial aid or how to find the time to do the homework; just take the first step in identifying three possible schools that make sense and ordering their catalogues to compare them side by side.

Creating Your Outer Circle of Life

Once you have identified these small action steps, write them on the outer ring of the circle, right by the slice to which they pertain. Make sure these steps are very specific. For example, losing weight is a general idea or goal, but you are looking for a specific action such as "lose five pounds." Walking twenty minutes three times a week is an action step. "Change my diet" is too general, but "make breakfast at home" instead of buying junk food for breakfast is a specific action step. Don't try to change every aspect of your life-long eating pattern. Make one change. You might "drink water instead of soda." Just that one change can have a significant impact on your physical and mental health.

These next steps are common-sense steps. If you are not sleeping enough, go to bed earlier. If you're not drinking enough water, the obvious next step is to drink more. The point is not to make this "next step" process mysterious or difficult. As you step back from the issue and see the whole picture, you can allow yourself to naturally sense the next simple action step.

Look at each of the areas of your circle and think of this next phase as stepping up your life. You're giving yourself a tune-up by identifying simple steps that point you in the right direction. One tune-up can make the whole car run smoother and make the ride much more enjoyable.

It can be very beneficial to have a supportive friend, partner, or even a support group when you are making life changes. If you have these resources in your life, be sure to let them know how they can support you in your process of change. If you don't have this support, make the changes anyway.

List Your Small Action Steps on One Page

Putting the small action steps you plan to take on one page in the outer circle allows you to see them all together. This becomes a map for how you are going to move your life to the next level. Your Circle of Life might have only three or four action steps at first. As you start to feel the natural momentum to move forward to your more positive future, you can add more steps later. Or you can prioritize them, perhaps by just focusing on one or two areas at first, then building in more changes as you develop excitement and enthusiasm for your new life.

If you wish, you can add action steps to all the slices in your life, even the "plus" slices. This gives you an ongoing action plan for how to progress with your steps. Whenever you are ready to take another step forward, you can refer to your Circle of Life and pick the next action step you are ready to take. There are always opportunities to progress, and it is easier to know what is next when you have all the options in front of you.

Whatever age you are right now, it's never too late for you to raise the quality of your life by filling the slices that need to be filled with more joyful activities, and emptying the slices that are overburdened.

It's your life. No one else can fix it but you!

Here's an example of the importance of understanding which slice in your life really needs the attention. One client, Carly, had moved with her husband to a new city and hadn't managed to replace her girlfriends back home. She was constantly trying to get her husband to have "girlfriend talk" with her, and he was always just responding with advice or boredom. Then she would criticize him for not listening, when he was really overwhelmed with the level of detail that she wanted to impart. The problem was not with her husband. The problem was that her "friendship slice" was empty, and she was trying to get her husband to play a part in her life that really didn't fit him. Once she realized this, overnight she stopped having these chronic arguments, while she began to work on finding a girlfriend to chat with. Soon she began having lunch once a week with her new friend Lakeisha. Lakeisha was also interested in doing a Circle of Life, so over lunch they talked about how they were progressing, and this regular conversation really helped Carly feel more supported.

It is important to notice exactly where the imbalance is occurring. Then you can begin to take actions that are able to address the problem, because now you have correctly identified the cause. Otherwise, you may be trying to fix the wrong problem, as Carly was when she tried to get her husband to act like a girlfriend.

As you look at your completed Circle of Life, you can review it from the perspective that comes from having an "overview." You can see where there are a lot of crowded slices, and where there are empty slices. Maybe you hadn't even noticed that hobbies, for example, were an empty area of your life.

This was what Darryl noticed when he looked over his completed circle. He was trying to figure out how to have less stress in his life, and this was the first thing he saw. He wasn't spending any time on activities that recharged his battery. He remembered how much he loved hitting golf balls and started going out after dinner to the driving range. For him this was instant serenity. It was the one time his brain was not trying to solve the problems of the day. He found he started sleeping better, which made him less irritable during the day and more able to find elegant solutions at work.

Another client, Elise, was a screenwriter. When she looked at her completed Circle of Life, she had an interesting insight. In screenwriting there is a technical term for a story called "The Mid-Point." This is a dramatic turning point in a movie—it can be good or bad—for the hero or heroine. This occurs around the middle of the movie, and it shapes the rest of the story. As Elise looked at her Circle, she felt she was at a Mid-Point. She was putting too much time into her career and not enough time on her spirituality, or her emotional and physical life. She realized it was an important time to turn her life around and create some balance. Her sister had died of a heart attack at 61. Elise realized it was time for her to correct her course, reconnect to her Higher Power, and reclaim her balance for the years ahead.

Create Your Compelling Future

In Part Two of this book we will explore how to contemplate your perfect future. This is where you create a compelling future so clearly in your mind that it draws you like a magnet towards everything you want in your beautiful Circle of Life.

CHAPTER 5

How to Use Your Intention to Experience Desired Changes

The next step in working with your Circle of Life process is exciting, because you are now ready to begin to use it as a tool to move forward. In the first steps, when you were creating your circle, you disciplined your mind to stay focused on the present—on what is happening right now. Now the next step is to take a mental quantum leap into the future—that is, the future not simply as a continuation of what you are doing today. Now you are going to use your imagination to create the future as you want it to be. You will use the power of your mind's ability to imagine yourself achieving your desired goals, as well as to see your future exactly the way you would like it to be.

Using your mind's tremendous power for imagining, you create the changes first as an image/feeling/perception—and then use this momentum to draw you like a magnet to the future you truly desire. Mentally and emotionally, you allow your thoughts and imaginings to visualize and move you into the future. Remember, this is not the future of more of the same, because, if you just take the same actions, you will just get the same results. Instead, you imagine the future as you would ideally like it to be. In other words, just imagine if all or most of your slices were pluses: how would that feel? What would your life be like? Can you imagine how that would feel? Use this strong intention to draw your future to you now.

It is important to begin creating in your awareness a more positive future, to help you move toward this reality. Truly let yourself imagine this. Don't skip this step, because this is how you make it real, by seeing it in your mind and feeling it in your body first. This is your opportunity to really allow yourself to live at your fullest potential.

One client, Alicia, was at first intimidated when I told her to imagine what her life would be like if it were all pluses. "I'd have nothing left to do if I was perfect." The truth is there are always new desires and goals to aspire to. You then can move to the next level of desire and growth. This is how your circle becomes an expanding spiral. When you achieve all your goals, you set new ones. You start a new Circle of Life. In this way you are in a constant process of becoming happier and more fulfilled. Now you are building on a foundation of happiness and satisfaction, and that fuels your willingness to pursue an even greater destiny.

This step, imagining (sometimes called visualizing) your life as all pluses, exercises your imagination. There is a great benefit in fully letting yourself experience what your life would be like if you made some of these changes. The best way to do this is to imagine yourself completely in the new experience. Use all your senses to see, hear, and feel what this new life would be like. This is better than simply observing yourself as on a movie screen. If you incorporate all your senses, then your imagination will have more force and effectiveness. Can you imagine living at the center of this new reality with your whole life at this higher level? Some people find this step really exciting. This is an important technique, because what you can imagine you can begin to move toward and make real in your life. As the saying goes, "What you can perceive, you can achieve."

Remember, I mentioned earlier about taking small, common-sense steps to move you in the direction you want to go. If thinking about a certain step makes you feel more aligned, connected, or on track with your purpose, it is the right step. As I have said, the advantage of smaller steps is that they are manageable, are easy to achieve, and won't short-circuit your momentum the way a huge leap might.

If your mind races too far ahead in the future, it may cause you to feel demoralized, because you can't find the path with simple, concrete action steps. It is good to have a "big vision" of where you want to go, but you want to make sure you don't get stuck in the gap between where you are and where you want to end up. If your mind starts spinning out, focusing on the distance between where you are in this moment and where you want to be, you could end up feeling defeated and not even take that first step. It can create an uncomfortable feeling of dissonance between where you are in this moment and where you want to be. The fastest way to move forward is to have a fundamental acceptance and recognition of where you are, as well as what simple steps will move you onward. This is why I have suggested simple, small, and obvious or common-sense steps, so that you can build momentum.

Now that you understand the importance of not getting too far ahead of yourself, you can begin to use your creative imagination as a blueprint helping you to make your plan concrete. Having a clear vision of what it would look like, sound like, feel like, will make it easier for you to stay focused on taking the right actions that lead to change.

Imagining your life, feeling how you would feel—as if these changes were already made—can be the fuel that gets you going and keeps you going. This image of a more perfect future is what gives you the juice to make the changes you need to make today. Your small efforts towards what you want to have in your future is exercising your intention. Learning how to use your mind in this way gives you strength and determination to keep choosing your goals each moment. At some point your larger goals will be achieved through the gradual accomplishment of your smaller steps.

Getting Started With Your Imaginative Process

Begin by being in a relaxed setting. That could be in nature, by a stream, or at home with soothing music. Any place where you can relax and spend a half-hour or so of uninterrupted time will be good. Give yourself permission to have this "me time." Nothing is more important than taking this time to contemplate how you want your life to be.

Use your breath to quiet the mind. Often just three slow, deep breaths will naturally help you get into that relaxed state of mind. If you have your own method, use that. Or if you want a suggestion for a breathing technique, you might try this method: Breathe deeply into your abdomen, not your chest for a slow count of five for each inhale and exhale. In between each inhale/exhale, hold or pause for a count of five. Using this method will slow your breath into a deeper pattern.

You can use that breathing practice, or any other meditation processes you use, to allow yourself to settle into a peaceful place inside. Some people like to close their eyes for a few minutes to help their brain move into the relaxed brain wave states. Peak achievers in business, sports, and other high performance activities have all learned that how you direct your own mind is the secret to success in any endeavor.

There are many good methods for using the breath to put you into an optimal or relaxed state of mind. Experiment with different techniques and see which ones work best for you. Any rhythmic breathing pattern will be useful.

Once you are in a relaxed mental and physical state, begin to use your imagination, just as if there were a movie in your mind, as many star athletes do before a major sports event. Actually see yourself performing perfectly in your chosen area. For some people, this is a visual experience; they can literally see themselves. For others, they can feel the sensations or hear the sounds. Use any and all senses that evoke the experience you wish to have as if it were real and true right now. How does this new reality feel? Continue to open your mind to these possibilities as you imagine yourself living and experiencing new activities or reaching new goals.

Your creative imagination is building a neural pathway pointing your mind in the right direction. Feel the confidence, trust, and belief in yourself at this new level. Feel that way now, even though you have not accomplished this in the outer world. Let your inner world build the muscle or the template which will allow for change to manifest. This is how you move from one level to another—you literally "change your mind." Then energy follows thought, and you are on your way!

Take as much time as you need for this step—to see, feel, hear, and sense yourself at this new level. Imagine how you would look and sound if you were already there. Perceive yourself as if you had already made the changes. The more real you make this in your mind, the more force or "mind power" there is to attract the right people and actions into your new positive zone of experience.

You are creating a mental experience or visualization. Doing this often will make it stronger. Do it while you are doing the dishes, taking a shower, engaging in almost any activity. The more you do it, the more power this new vision or sensation gains and the more it becomes a driving force in your life.

To help get started, you can ask yourself these questions:

- If I made this specific change (fill in the blank), how would I feel?
- What would my new life be like?

The more specific your answers are, the more these images will help you create a compelling future to move toward. The Circle of Life is a process of continual fine-tuning until your life is where you want it to be. Visualizing, imagining, or meditating on your perfect future can draw you magnetically to become everything you want to be.

Your Goal Circle—The Map for Where You Want to Go

The outer ring of your circle is your goal circle. It is where you write the positive changes you are willing to make. This outer ring is the map leading you exactly where you want to go. You can also make this Goal Circle as a separate page that lists all your positive goals with the dates you would like to achieve them. Put this circle where you will see it every day, such as on your bathroom mirror, on your smart phone, or any place else you look for inspiration. This will help motivate you and keep you on purpose.

It's your Circle of Life. Design it any way you want, and imagine it taking you anywhere you want to go.

Circle of Life

Name _____

Date _____

- Physical Health
- Mental Health Self Esteem
- Relaxation Stress Management
- Hobbies
- Exercise
- Friends Co-workers
- Diet
- Family Origin
- Sleep
- Significant Other
- Home
- Children
- Pets
- Spirituality
- Education/Training
- Goals, Dreams, Aspirations
- Career/Job
- Finances

+	
✔	
−	

Here are some examples from patients working on this step of turning their goals into reality:

Sheila wanted to get more sleep, so she visualized the clock in a dark room showing 10 P.M. Then she visualized a bright room showing 7:30 A.M. Within a month, her body started to move into this rhythm on its own. When she began to feel really tired around 10 P.M., she chose to pay attention to that and go to sleep. Instead of overriding her body's messages, she began to move into sync with her own rhythm. It wasn't long before she noticed she was sleeping through the night more frequently.

Alice wanted to have more friends in her life. She saw herself surrounded by two or three others, doing some of the fun things she wanted to do. Two weeks later a friend at work invited her on a hike, and she then joined the hiking club, which led to several more enjoyable invitations.

John wanted to change his relationship to money. He saw himself putting a hundred dollars a month into his IRA. He created a budget he could live by. As a reward for following his budget, he let himself spend any "extra" on pure splurges. After six months, he was able to stick by his own rules, and each month he had a little bit of "mad money" to play with.

Larry wanted to finish his degree. He bought the frame for the degree and put it on the wall with one word on the page—"Master's"—until he could get the degree. Seeing that image helped him make better choices when his friends wanted to side-track him with suggestions to "hang out."

Mona began collecting travel images from the many places she wanted to visit, and created a vision board of her itinerary. She answered an ad to teach English for an international company, which had listed four of the countries she had posted on her vision board. Within three months, she was on her way!

Using Your Imagination to Go to the Next Level

It has been well documented in numerous scientific studies that, when you visualize, you prepare your mind. When your mind is prepared, you tend to take the right action steps with greater ease. You are more likely to follow through with the steps once your mind has already seen the path. The power of visualization with intention is in your mind, and the results show up in every area of your life.

Exercise Your Positive Imagination Every Day

The imaginative process or visualizing your life exactly as you want it to be is not a one-time deal. The key to making the changes you would like to see is the repetitive process of building a new-brain habit by creating it as a mentally compelling experience every day just as you want your life to be. Visualization with intention sets the process in motion, and you must maintain the momentum. This is going to become your new commitment to yourself, to hold the vision through using positive self-talk, affirmations, and a creative approach to building your future. This is how you learn to have a creative reality instead of an accidental one. These skills are discussed in more detail in Part Two of this book.

Remember, I suggest small steps, because you are more likely to follow through with them. One of the fastest ways to build your self-esteem is to decide to do something—and then actually do it. It builds your own trust in your word, your integrity, and your strength of character. It takes determination to change, and following through builds confidence and personal will power.

For example, in working with the outer goal circle, let's say you made a small decision such as to go to bed a half-hour earlier, or drink one or two more glasses of water a day, or clean your desk once a week. Make sure you follow through with these steps. Following through with small steps builds motivation and momentum to make bigger changes.

If you're human and you make a decision to change some behavior, chances are some resistance is going to rear its head. This is natural, normal, and a part of the "action/reaction" factor. So, don't think you are doing it wrong if on Day One or Day Three or Twenty-three you suddenly don't want to make any of the wonderful changes you have promised yourself! This is just "the muscle of change," going through its cycle of stretching and contracting. Be gentle with your self-talk at this point—and just keep going for your goals!

As I've said, simple and specific changes are good, because, while you may resist the bigger action of eating healthy foods, you might be able to take a simple step such as getting yourself to drink one glass of water. Even if you are having an "I won't do it" tantrum, you can probably talk yourself into an easy step anyway—because you want to do the new behavior, and because you have made a promise to yourself.

Make the Changes that are Right for You

If your level of resistance is insurmountable, it could be that you have over- committed to a change that was either too big at this moment, or not really the one that you truly wanted to make. In order to make sincere commitments, you have to really want something authentic from the process. In other words, if you are trying to make a change because someone else believes it is important to you, but in your heart of hearts you don't really believe it is essential for your true well-being, you won't follow through. So be sure to check in with your own sense of truth before you commit to making changes.

Personal accountability builds when you say what you're going to do and then do it. If you discover it wasn't the right course of action for you, make another agreement that modifies the original. As you continue to commit to these actions, you begin to raise your sense of self-esteem. Your opinion of your ability to handle and enjoy life increases.

As you move through this process of committing and following through, you are also moving to a greater appreciation of the impact of your actions (and inactions) on your own life and on the lives of those connected to you. This process gently moves you into greater self-awareness and more conscious living.

One of the many benefits of visualizing where you want your circle to be in the future is that it teaches your mind to be more fluid and open to moving on. The mind can get stuck thinking that "what is" is what will always be. So the process of visualizing is a way to make the mind more flexible and open to possibility. Like your breath, which is always in a constant state of motion, your life is a work of art that is constantly moving.

Once you have done this Circle of Life process and are visualizing your future, I recommend that you check back with your circle every three to six months. One of my patients has her circle in her scheduling book, and often glances at it while she's making major decisions. Check again at nine months, and then a year later, or check in more often. The point is to check back and see what progress you have made. You can chart these changes in your outer circle or make another circle if you're making many changes and have new changes to add to your original chart. Be sure to date it so when you go back you know when you were working on these changes. If you feel like you have accomplished all your goals, you may choose to start making a new circle.

If you haven't made much progress in a certain area, you need to see why you haven't been willing to make small changes to move your life in the direction you thought you wanted to move. Perhaps the goals you thought were important are not the real ones that make your heart sing.

If you find that you have achieved the majority of your goals, and your scores are now mostly pluses or checks, it is probably time to make a brand new circle. Any time you tell the truth about your life and are willing to be in the present moment, you will have more access to your true personal power and will get a brand new start on your dreams!

CHAPTER 6

Filling vs. Emptying Your Circle of Life

As you step back and examine your completed Circle of Life, you may notice that there are certain patterns on the page. Some slices may have too much going on inside them; others may be blank or nearly so. It is at this point in the Circle of Life process that you get a sense of where you are too spread out, perhaps where you are doing too much for others or being run by other people's agendas. Conversely, there may be some areas of your life that are getting no energy or attention at all.

What you want to notice is in which areas of your life you need more balance. If your Circle is cluttered with way too much going on, you may want to see if you can begin to empty some areas, creating more space for your true priorities. This is the point where you take a look at everything you are doing and see if there are some areas of your life where you need to start saying "no." It is like emptying your cup to allow new energy to fill in what you really want to achieve and accomplish.

If you have identified one or more areas where you feel bombarded, overloaded, or imploded, it is time to think about creating space! This begins with making choices about how you are going to spend your time, your energy, and your focus. The beautiful irony of this process is that you may have to do some emptying in order to live a more fulfilling life. If your Circle is too crowded, it will block or inhibit new growth. This process takes trust that, if you start saying "no," it will make a space for a new and better "yes." Only you know if you need to slim down your Circle of Life, or what areas need trimming to make space for higher priorities.

Sometimes important people in your life can give you needed perspective about what changes would be good for you. Other times, you have to follow your own gut sense about what is right for you. This requires a certain discrimination to know what your truth is. This weeding-out process is unique to you, so in this case, resist the temptation to get "advice" from someone else, because the area that one person may need to empty is the same area someone else may need to fill.

In order to optimize your life, you are going to have to reduce clutter, that is, habitual or unproductive activities. Trust that if you stop pouring energy in one direction, you will create more energy for a higher priority area.

This is Your Precious Life

It may feel scary or you might even feel guilty if you start pulling back your energy in certain areas. This is your precious life, so choose what you want in it!

One of the most important things you can do in designing your life to be the way you want it to be is to stop spending your energy in areas that don't truly serve you. It is a process of refining or streamlining. This is the weeding phase, where you are pulling up the time suckers to make more room for the flowers of your truest personal expression. It is one of the best things you can do, if you want to move quickly to the next and best phase of your life. If you take this time to rebalance, you will make the right space for the new changes you truly desire. When you free up time, energy, and focus, the areas of true priority begin to flourish, and your spirit will be strengthened in the process!

See Your Circle Every Day

It is a good idea to stay visually connected to your circle. I remind my patients to put it where they can see it often. If you keep it in a notebook, be sure to revisit it from time to time or at key moments such as your birthday, New Year's Eve, or any significant time reference you might have. If you feel comfortable, put it on your wall or bulletin board, where you will see it every day. It is very powerful to keep it in your daily line of vision.

You may have some ideas about how this process could help family or partners. For some people it can be very useful to share this process with family, friends, or a significant other. It can be illuminating to understand differences in each of your styles or priorities, and thus it can enable you all to work together more effectively and harmoniously. When you each understand what is truly important to the other, communication becomes cleaner and more rewarding.

Another application of this process is to use it to focus on a particular area in greater detail. You can use the Circle of Life process to support your growth in the specific area that is important to you. For example, if you want to make a major lifestyle change such as introducing healthy eating and exercising, you may want to make an entire circle devoted to exploring all the elements of this particular issue.

Some people like to use the Circle of Life process in specific time contexts such as in intervals of three-, six-, or nine-month plans. What would you like your life to look like in the next few months? You can use the Circle of Life to chart the course of your life over specific time intervals.

How Your Change Affects Others

If you are in a situation in life where you are responsible for others—children, elderly parents, or extended family—you may have duties and obligations. In some cultures, the overall balance and harmony of the family may be considered more important than the needs of individuals to chart their own course. If you come from a multi-cultural family, you may have conflicting values pulling on you. Family responsibilities may put limitations on your personal time, which may mean that you have to be patient with your own desires for growth and change.

If this is the case, pace yourself. The rate of change you make may need to take into consideration the needs of others. Be patient with your progress. Perhaps at another point in time you will have more freedom and liberty to determine your own fate.

Your Life as a Work of Art

Congratulations on completing your first Circle of Life. Perhaps you are gaining a clearer focus and more awareness about what is most important to you. I hope this process has given you more insight into where you want to go from here.

Putting your Circle of Life down on paper gives you a marker for change, so you can map your progress as you move through life. You can keep track of the various accomplishments and achievements that can inspire you to set new goals and create experiences you wish to have.

This is only the beginning of your potential for using the Circle of Life for total life transformation. For those of you interested in further explorations and creative applications, in Part Two of this book I will show you some of the additional ways you can apply the Circle of Life. For example, to heal from past relationships, improve current ones, or to create new behaviors and patterns for healthier relating, experiment with the Relationship Circle described in Part Two.

There is no limit to how wonderful your life could become. Use your imagination to guide you on how to use this Circle of Life process to transform your life into a true work of art!

Tanya's Story

Tanya came into therapy after her third abortion. She was waiting tables; felt overwhelmed by her unpaid bills, and felt she had no spiritual connection and no support in her life. She had abandoned her dream of designing clothes. She lived with three roommates, and her own room was a total mess—which was just how she felt about her life.

She decided that her first action step of good self-care was getting her room cleaned up. She realized she couldn't handle all her big problems, but her fifteen-by-twenty-foot room, which was her working and living space, felt like it needed to be her first action step. She decided to spend just two hours a day cleaning and organizing. Realizing that she hated the pale pea-green color that had been there since she moved in, she took it upon herself to repaint the room. She chose a lilac and cream combination, and these colors lifted her spirits and energy immediately. She set up a small altar in one corner, with inspiring goddess images. She set up her computer and sewing machine along another wall, and the sense of order renewed her spirit.

For the first time in years, her room began to feel like her sanctuary. Instead of just spending every night hanging out with her roommates in the living room watching TV and eating fast food, ending up feeling that she had wasted another night, she found she loved her quiet evenings, listening to music and working on sewing purses in her beautiful, serene room.

Next she began jogging again. She started taking birth control pills and got on a better eating regimen. All these changes took less than a month, and her sewing was really inspiring her. She was delighted when her roommates bought some of her hand-made purses for themselves and as gifts, and she began to see how she could turn this into a small business. Her first goal was to update her portfolio, and from there to develop her website showing her custom-made purses. Although she still had major life issues to resolve, she now felt she trusted herself to handle them, one step at a time.

Part Two

∼

Using Your
Circle of Life Process
to Re-Design Your Future

The Skills You Need To Help
You Get the Most Out of Your Circle of Life

CHAPTER 7

Using the Power of Affirmations to Change Your Behavior

How you talk to yourself inside your head, or what you say out loud, will have a large impact on how you feel about yourself as well as what you think about yourself. If you are constantly thinking self-critical words and statements, it is going to hamper your effectiveness in the world. Because what you think about, you bring about. So, this is a good time to "tune up" your brain with more positive self-talk!

One of the quickest ways to bring about change in the kinds of experiences you are attracting to yourself is to begin to use positive self-talk or affirmations. New behavior often begins with talking to yourself in new ways—new positive self-talk leads naturally to new thoughts, feelings, beliefs, and actions.

If you are not aware of your own self-talk, begin to pay attention to the words and phrases you say to yourself throughout the day. Are these mostly positive and encouraging words running through your mind, or even out of your mouth? Do they support you to feel and do your best? Do you have an inner coaching team that encourages you to keep going and succeed?

Or do you have a series of inner critics who judge you at every turn? You may have internalized a parent, an authority figure, or society's standards, and those critical words bang around in your brain like a dizzy boxer in a boxing ring. You may literally hear this as someone else's words in your head, or you may not even remember where you got those negative ideas. It doesn't matter where they came from; what matters is that you begin to recognize the force they have had in your mind and in your life.

If you are like most people, you will be surprised to discover how much negative self-talk runs on automatic. The first step is to become aware of this talk. That is how you break down the powerful grip it has on your every waking moment. The next step is to use the same mental process, in a positive manner. In other words, we can't turn off thinking, but we can think more productively. That's where affirmations come in.

Affirmations are a way to connect with our inner positivity. They allow us to create mental pathways that cause new behavior to unfold naturally. Affirmations can help you make better and healthier choices and create your life just the way you want it to be.

When our inner voice is congruent, meaning our thoughts are a match with our desires, they have more creative power. Contradictory thoughts (such as desires combined with the fear that you can't achieve those desires) split your life force, and these divided thoughts reduce your effectiveness. Repetition of any thought creates more focus, intensity, and clarity. As with a muscle, the more you use an affirmation, the stronger it gets.

When you first say an affirmation it may not even feel true or real to you. For example, if you have no time for fun in your life, and you start with a simple affirmation of: "I have time for play in my life," the first time you say it, it may feel like a bold-faced lie!

What this statement does is shine a light on the fact that you haven't been making a space for fun. Next, if you begin to repeat it, it starts to gather some force of attraction, and this helps you begin to focus on fun. Once you concentrate on the *possibility of fun,* you begin to be attracted to opportunities that lead you in that direction. Soon you are making choices that honor that desire.

Affirmations Guide You to Where You Want to Go

Your affirmation is like a road map to where you want to go. It doesn't mean that, the first time you say it, you're there. Although, if you say it with total conviction, that is possible! What an affirmation ordinarily does is lead you to where you want to go, and it helps guide you when you are faced with choices or forks in the road. When you test a potential decision against your affirmation, you can feel whether the left or right fork leads you toward or away from the intent of your affirmation. For example, let's say you are working on having more fun in your life and someone tries to enlist you in a big project. Test it against your affirmation. See if it intuitively feels that it leads you toward or away from fun. Even if it is a noble project, it may not be the best choice for you at this time. In this way, affirmations can help us navigate the twists and turns of life.

Affirmations work best if they are stated in short sentences. The brain focuses better and the affirmation has more power if it has only one core idea to deal with. In other words "I have time in my life for fun" will be more effective than a longer sentence with multiple ideas. Here is an example of trying to put too many ideas in an affirmation: "I make the best choices as to whom I spend time with in order to have more fun and balance in my life." These are all good idea concepts, just too many of them in one affirmation, and they will not resonate as well in the brain. It is like trying to sing three songs at once.

It's better to separate complex ideas into distinct statements such as "I make the best choices as to whom I spend time with," and "I feel more balanced in my life." This is better than trying to put fun, balance, and choices all in the same affirmation.

Affirmations need to be stated in the positive. Say what it is you do want, not what you don't want. If you say "I have no more fear in my life," you are saying the word "fear" to your brain, which reminds the brain of fear. There is such a practiced pathway there that, within nanoseconds, your brain is producing ten reasons why you should be afraid. A more effective affirmation would be, "I feel bold about my future career."

Make sure to state your affirmations in the present tense, as above, rather than say "I will feel bold . . . ." Affirmations work best in the present tense, and this tricks the brain into believing they are possible *right now*!

Just a friendly reminder—be realistic about your affirmation. In other words, if you have an affirmation that says "I am happy all the time," that is a set-up for failure, because nobody is happy ALL the time. That affirmation may sound nice when you first hear it, and it has a good intention within it; however, it can cause you to feel that you failed if one day you find you just aren't happy. Then you might think you haven't achieved anything, even if you've been happier for the past three days. A more effective affirmation could be something like this: "I allow more happiness in my life." That creates less resistance or backlash, and it also allows for the normal experience of not being happy every second.

Make sure when you are creating your affirmations that you choose those that are in alignment with what you want. Make sure the affirmations match your true values. Otherwise, like a shirt that is way too big, they just hang around your shoulders, annoying you.

Affirmations are the next step in Your Circle of Life process. Pick any slice where you want to have a deep focus or major transformation. You can make a list of your own affirmations or borrow some that I suggest later in this chapter. A good affirmation should excite you. Affirmations may feel a little scary because they are a stretch to your brain, but they should "ring true." Work on changing the words until there is a sense of the "perfect fit." Having the right words should feel like it all "clicks in" for you. Sometimes it takes some refining and revising to get the sentence just right, and this helps you to get really clear about what you want. When you find the right words, they shine like a polished diamond, so take the time to refine until you feel the affirmation is perfect for you.

Affirmations can be extremely powerful to add to your Circle of Life to make it a comprehensive tool for total life transformation. Make your affirmation gentle and clear.

When you work with an affirmation, don't force it. It is not about unrelenting repetition. Relax; allow it to work its magic, like warm water flowing over you. Think of tenderly receiving the energy of the affirmation.

Here are some suggested affirmations that have been useful to other patients; of course, feel free to make up your own that personally inspire you.

Some Sample Affirmations:

I feel great when I take time for myself.

Money allows me freedom.

Great ideas come to me easily.

I love making healthy choices.

When I do what I love, happiness comes my way.

Enjoy the ride!

Remember to be creative, making up your own affirmations until you find ones that perfectly match your desires. You can feel it in your body and mind if what you are saying isn't true for you. Just keep searching until you find a statement of affirmation that matches your true feelings and is the right expression of what you want in your life.

Gabby's Story

Gabby was working as a waitress and a dog walker when she came into therapy. For twenty years she had wanted to be a screenwriter, and she had finally won a small screenwriting contest. In her years of writing she had so many disappointments that she was afraid to enjoy this potential victory, even though the prize was a round-trip ticket and hotel stay at a writers' conference in Maui. She had the idea that to speak about her recent success would "jinx it." She was afraid to try affirmations because, as she put it, "I just can't handle one more disappointment if the affirmation doesn't come true."

I suggested she just start with something simple that didn't trigger her past memories of repeated failures. We worked with the wording until we came up with the affirmation: "I allow myself to have a new level of success." Just hearing those words cheered her up and made her feel motivated to take some actions she needed to take in terms of self-promotion.

Instead of dreading the competitive nature of the conference, she began to look forward to it with a new confidence she hadn't felt in years. She made a commitment to be open to new and positive possibilities and to have fun, even though the schedule of workshops was grueling. She stuck with the positive feelings her affirmation generated for her. She thoroughly enjoyed the experience of the conference—and she met and fell in love with a man who was the kind of partner she had barely allowed herself to imagine. He was an agent's assistant, and he helped her get her foot in the door.

Now Gabby is a big believer in planning for positive change through the use of focusing her mind on positive potential. "I used to use my mind to imagine the worst. I might as well use that same power to imagine the best."

CHAPTER 8

Enhancing Your Self-Esteem to Create the Life of Your Dreams

Almost everyone who comes into counseling with me has some level of self-doubt and feelings of not being "good enough." Their lowered self-esteem is one of the things that keep them from achieving their goals and dreams. Then this further lowers their sense of self because they are convinced they are not doing well enough in their life. If low self-esteem is an issue for you, the first thing I can tell you is—*you are not alone*! So many people struggle in our society with this issue, it is virtually at epidemic proportions!

The problem with low self-esteem is that it can stunt your growth because you stop reaching for your full potential, because you think you can't or don't deserve greater success and happiness. This then leads to saying "no" to opportunities or possibilities for choices that might improve your life. These feelings blind you to the good you could be doing in the world. Or the healthy and fun relationships you could have. Or the pleasure you could experience.

For some people this relates to a specific area where they believe they are not succeeding. We all have areas in which we think we are weak—for example, it could be math, intimate relationships, housekeeping, or exercise. When this self-doubt spills into multiple areas, it can result in lowering your self-esteem, leading to generalized feelings of not being worthy or lovable.

Your level of self-esteem determines how you *feel* about yourself. Your self-concept, on the other hand, refers to how you *think* about yourself. For example, thinking you are not smart enough can lead to a low self-concept and cause you to not pursue a better job. This distinction between a thought about yourself and a feeling about yourself may seem subtle or arbitrary at first. It can be a really useful tool if you are in a situation where you feel conflicted and need to understand the source of this self-doubt.

One example to illustrate this issue of feeling conflicted is when people want to break up with their partner and their head has all the reasons why they should break up, but their heart wants to stay connected to that person. This creates a conflict between the thoughts and the feelings.

The challenge in this case is to integrate the thoughts and feelings, in order to know whether or not breaking up is the right decision. Ask yourself if you generally make decisions based on your thoughts or your feelings. Or do you make them based on an integrated approach? Having a split between the heart and the mind is the cause of much suffering. This is why understanding the distinction between your thoughts and your feelings, and learning how to unite and integrate them, is so important.

If you are feeling a lot of conflict between these two areas, it may be possible that you are picking up and responding to this split in your partner's heart and mind. Sometimes sensing this conflict in a loved one can trigger our own feelings of being separated. It's important to become aware of your thoughts and feelings and work them through until you feel more integrated between the different sides of yourself. This is your next step in order to fully commit to your partner.

Steve, a new patient, was just becoming aware of his thoughts and the almost constant self-critical chatter in his brain.

"Where do these incredibly negative ideas come from?" Steve asked. Sometimes the critical voices come from external standards you have internalized. For example, they may come from ideas learned, or experiences with your family, or in school, or from authority figures. It really doesn't matter where you learned these negative ideas; what matters is that you understand that, once you gain awareness of how you are keeping this negative habit going, you can begin to change it. The really good news here is that negative self-concept as well as low self-esteem is reversible conditions!

It is important to get to work on cleaning up these old negative ideas you have repeating in your brain, because they can affect you even when you experience success. One patient who just won an important state election said that the day after the victory he felt the worst he had ever felt. All his insecurities came to the surface. He felt like a phony and was plagued with self-doubt. It was clear that, no matter how much he had achieved, it didn't erase how he felt about himself deep down inside. In therapy I got him to reconnect with his genuine desire to serve the public, and to remind himself that he had the skills and expertise to do it. He got himself back on track so he could start using his brilliant mind to focus on the positive work ahead.

Your self-concept is what you think about yourself and your achievements. Take a moment to make a list of all the things you have achieved, large and small: the degrees earned, the merit badges or recognition received, the tasks you have finished, the goals you set and accomplished. Just making this list can remind you of how much you have achieved. If you are finding no more than three achievements, it means you are not giving yourself much credit.

Our sense of self-esteem shows up in the decisions we make every day. It is the reputation we hold of ourselves. If we are telling ourselves things like "You're not good enough, you'll never succeed at . . . .," we most likely will not even try, or if we do, we will mess it up in order to subconsciously prove that the negative thoughts were right. In this way, negative self-perception affects the small and large choices we make every day.

Reversing low self-esteem is done in small, consistent steps. The first step is to catch or notice your self-talk and negative feelings and low self-esteem, as these can cause you to make a decision based on a skewed perception of who you are.

One shy client, Mark, went out to a party at a neighbor's one night. There he saw a woman whom he found attractive. He noticed he was frozen by the thought "I can't go over and talk to her. She probably doesn't want anyone bothering her." He was able to notice this thought and he was able to switch it by telling himself something else: "I really won't know if she wants to talk to me—unless I say hello. She might want to talk." Just changing that one thought led him to a more positive, self-affirming decision.

Mark thought his feelings were so deeply ingrained that he couldn't change them. It was liberating for him when he understood that feelings and thoughts are just energy. They change all the time. He just needed to learn *how* to change them. He began to learn how to harness the energy and reverse its direction.

If a thought comes to mind, listen to it. Does it ring true? If not, dispute it. Keep letting go of thoughts that don't serve you until you come up with thoughts that inspire and motivate you. When you find a positive thought, give it your energy, power and focus. The idea is to work with this new, true thought and let it resonate throughout your life.

The reason it is important to take back control of your thoughts is that every single decision or choice you make is based on your current sense of self. You begin to reverse negative self-concepts every time you talk differently to yourself, and you then make small, better decisions based on these new positive directions.

For example, let's say you are saying to yourself: "I can't dance." That may be a true fact. If it is important to you not to miss out on the fun of dancing, you can take a beginner's dance class. Sign up for the class including this point of view; just don't let it stop you from taking action. You might say something like "I can't dance, but that is okay, because I can learn to dance." That statement is true, and it gives you the room and support to actually show up at a dance class.

If you are plagued with feelings of loneliness, take small action steps that will put you in the presence of other people doing something you enjoy doing, even if it involves small and simple interactions. In other words, take small actions that are the *opposite* of the beliefs that come from low self-esteem. If you continue to be led by the same old emotions, you will get the same results, keeping your life in lock-down. If you want to feel different, you are going to have to take different actions, which will lead to new and enhanced feelings about yourself and your life.

This begins a positive spiral upward toward higher self-esteem, where you start to build an increasing confidence in what you are capable of, and this inspires you to take new, positive steps. When self-defeating behavior is no longer running your life, you can begin to follow your heart's desires.

Instead of making lesser choices, you begin to live the "hero's or heroine's journey" (to use Joseph Campbell's terms) toward greater accomplishments and expressing your true potential.

The more you work with your Circle of Life, especially over time, the more it will tap into deeper layers of meaning and give you access to parts of your unconscious mind. Earlier I mentioned "the shadow," which is what Carl Jung called our unconscious self, where we are unaware, denying or repressing aspects of ourselves. This shadow is our unknown or hidden self. We are often not in touch with this side of ourselves, and as we bring it forward into our awareness it can help us move ahead. This is because the shadow side diverts energy and pulls us toward it, drawing us like a magnet, even when our conscious mind has other plans and intentions. The shadow may pull you off-course!

One way to gain greater control over your actions and impulses is to integrate your shadow side. The shadow side may show up as an addiction. Or it can turn into shame about some area of your life, such as your opinion about your body, intelligence, or previous choices. The shadow side represents the parts of your life you don't want to acknowledge. Or it could be areas that you don't want to think about because you'll experience negative feelings. It can be challenging to face these issues, because they bring up feelings and memories that we are not wanting to accept or deal with. Once we realize, however, that we can heal and accept these parts of ourselves, we can then open ourselves to more energy and expansion of who we are.

Instead of letting the shadows operate from behind the scenes, if you integrate it into your conscious awareness, you will function more as "one mind." When the shadow is unrecognized, it has more control and runs many decisions and actions. When you recognize the shadow and integrate it into the other parts of your conscious mind, you then have all your ducks marching in a row, and you are much more effective at everything you do.

This is why there is great value in integrating your shadow side by bringing it forward as a part of your personality. You can then use all this power to bring your life together and experience more of your full potential.

As you begin to integrate your shadow self, it raises your self-esteem. The more you cultivate positive self-regard, the more you generate compassion, understanding, and kindness towards yourself. It is really delightful to begin hearing these voices inside your head: "You did really well . . ." or "You're a loving person . . ." or "You deserve to be happy . . . ." If you start saying affirmative words to yourself with more consistency and kindness, you will start to believe and accept them, and then express them in all areas of your life.

Carol was a nurse who worked ten-hour shifts. In order to take lunch or other breaks, she would have to make sure another nurse was covering for her, but she had such low self-esteem that she couldn't ask for the breaks she should have taken. After a week of repeating the simple positive statement, "I deserve the same breaks everyone else gets," she was able to speak up to her supervisor and ask for her breaks. This doesn't mean that in one week her self-esteem issues were entirely resolved, but it gave her hope that she could continue to work on her issue.

So start anywhere you can, by noticing perhaps one negative thought, and get to work on reversing it with its positive opposite. Repeat it often, with conviction, even if these are new thoughts for you. This is how you start to handcraft your own life and take back control of your thoughts.

Start right now. You'll be so happy that you did!

CHAPTER 9

Reclaiming Your Zest for Life through Creativity

Your creativity is the source of all the ways in life that you express your thoughts and feelings. It is your way of being uniquely yourself in the world. Whenever you bring something new into your life that is useful or innovative, you are expressing your creativity. Obviously, all forms of artistic expression—music, dance, art, photography, writing, crafts—are aspects of your creative expression. Expand this framework to include all the ways that you put your personal energetic fingerprint on any activity, thought, or feeling. Include how you bake a cake, how you compose a photo, how you cheer up a friend, how you arrange flowers, the colors you choose to wear, the way you solve a problem or throw a party, or how you make a living space your own.

Creativity is an approach to life. It is your zest or your personal pizzazz. If you feel this is missing in your life, or that it could be turned up, then all you have to do is nurture it. Your creativity will naturally unfold.

One quick way to reclaim your creativity is to ask yourself, "What makes me happy?" This will lead you back to your personal creativity and expression. Although children are naturally creative, as a grown-up you have one advantage—you have the delightful possibility of being able to do what you want. You don't have to wait for someone to tell you what to do, or give you permission to do it. For some people, this freedom can be intimidating or just too vague. Those who feel "creatively challenged" need to jumpstart their inner sense of fun. Keep asking yourself, "What makes me feel happy?" If you haven't asked yourself this in a while, be patient if the answer isn't immediately forthcoming. Keep asking! If your creativity has been on hold, it may feel like a shy girl at a dance; you may have to ask her more than once before she smiles and says "Yes."

Creativity is your personal expression in the world—if you exist, you are creative. You either have your creativity turned up or turned down, and it is possible to turn your creative dial *way up* in order to manifest more and more fulfilling forms of personal expression.

In your first explorations with the Circle of Life, you were looking at how your life is right now. In this part of the book, you are exploring your desire for change and taking a deeper look at the ways you can use your creativity to expand the quality of your life. Creativity is essential for a happy life. Take a look at any areas or slices of your life that you feel could benefit by a more creative approach and imagine how you can take them to the next level. Begin to imagine what a truly creative Circle of Life would look like. Let yourself paint outside the lines!

Using Our Creative Brain

We often refer to left-brain dominance as the side for logical or linear thinking. Without this side of our brain we couldn't balance our checkbooks, solve basic problems, or deal with linear time. When we refer to right-brain dominance functions, we are talking about our intuitive knowing, our emotions, our subtle perceptions, empathy, sensuality, creativity. So even if you don't imagine yourself being a "great artist," opening the flow of this side of yourself makes life feel more complete, more authentic, more passionate, and ultimately more human.

As children we are naturally creative, because it is a form of play, the only way of being in the world. As adults we often have to reclaim that side of ourselves in order to have more fun and "be more ourselves." Think of your creativity as your "play self." You may not be able to spend twenty-four hours a day expressing this side of yourself, but if you are spending no time during the week honoring, or even indulging, this aspect of yourself, you may feel burnt out, and life starts to lose its magic.

Take a realistic assessment of whether or not you are allowing yourself a reasonable "slice" of life for creativity. The amount needed for well-being is different for everyone. For some people a few minutes of day-dreaming while doing the dishes are enough. For others, unless they have a creative project going, or even a daily discipline of creative expression, life may feel as if it is being lived with the dimmer switch constantly turned down.

People's methods of becoming inspired and expanding their creativity are unique. You want to honor this process, and trust that there is a greater creative process at work, even if you feel you are not accessing it at the moment. Put your faith in the existence of this greater flow; this is the quickest way to gain your own path of entry. Since this is a unique inner journey, my recommendation would be that, if you can enjoy the journey, not only are you more likely to get some place interesting, but you will be expressing the creative energy of joy to fuel your ride!

Expand Your Definition of Creativity

I invite you to continually expand your definition of creativity until it becomes the unique approach you take to life. Bring creativity into your life in as many ways as possible. You can always find more creative ways to enhance every area of your life. Thus, think of creativity not just as a specific art project, but as a mode of living.

Here are some questions to get your "sense-process" going and to inspire you to nurture your unique creativity:

Questions to Jump Start Your Creativity

You can use these questions as a starting point by creating a special Creativity Circle of Life. These questions may inspire you to create specific slices. Or you can use these creativity "jump-starters" to add to one of your other circles.

- Am I nurturing my creativity? How? In what areas? What areas could I express myself in that I am not doing now?
- Do I feel inspired? Am I passionate about my creativity?
- If I had more time for creative expression, I would . . . (finish this sentence).
- Secretly, if nobody was looking or judging. I would love to be . . . . I would love to do . . . .
- If money were no object, I would spend more time . . . .
- If I could change or add a new vocation or profession other than what I do now, I would. . . .

- I am really moved by artists or people who . . . .
- When I was a child I used to love to . . . .
- Visual expressions, color, shape, texture, are really important to me. Colors that inspire me are . . . .
- Sounds, music . . . auditory elements that inspire me are. . . . My favorite kinds of music are . . . .
- Sports, dance, and forms of movement that inspire me are . . . .
- Words . . . writing . . . that inspire me are . . . .
- Movies, theater, performances that inspire me are . . . .
- Nature and nature sounds and images that inspire me are . . . .
- The top three artists or creative people that inspire me are . . . .
- Are there some limiting beliefs I have that interfere with fuller creative expression?
- What permission do I need to grant myself in order to cultivate my creativity?
- What are three simple action steps I could take to awaken or nurture my creativity?
- How am I creative in my relationships? Or could I be more creative?
- How am I creative with my goals, dreams, and aspirations?
- Am I creative in the ways I relax? How could I be more . . . ?
- Am I creative in my home? At work?
- Am I creative in school or learning?

- Am I creative in all the ways I could be?

Creative Affirmations

Here are some affirmations that my patients have used to help tame the inner critic and support creative expression.

- I am creative.
- I trust my personal creative process.
- I deserve to express myself fully.
- The way I do (...) is right for me.
- I am unique!
- I have a right to express myself.
- Freedom comes from owning my creativity.
- I am curious about my creative potential.
- I nurture my creative impulses and protect them from external judgment.
- I put energy into my creative process.
- I am willing to take creative risks.
- I love my creativity.
- I focus on my creativity.
- I enjoy the creative process.
- Creativity is fun!
- I allow myself to play!

Marvin's Story

Marvin had been married for eleven years when his wife shocked him with an e-mail telling him she was questioning whether or not she wanted to stay with him. Although he knew their passion had long since dwindled, they were so involved in their son's sports activities and seemed to the outside world to be such a perfect family, that this revelation literally felt like a bolt from the blue.

In looking at his Circle of Life, he realized that he had no "me" time. Everything he did was either work, taking care of repairs on their "fixer-upper house," or helping his ten-year-old son with homework "so he could get into a good college." In his mind, he felt like a dutiful husband and father, but he admitted that he and his wife Amy had not been on a date since their son was born. Marvin had married Amy straight out of college, and, although he could fix the faulty wiring in the old house, he had no idea how to fix a marriage.

Repairing his marriage was his first priority. He decided that his first simple action step would be to take his wife out to a nice restaurant and ask her, "What could I do to be a better husband?" He had never asked her anything like that, and he was almost as nervous as the night he proposed.

Amy was charmed by his flustering presentation of a red rose, and was so moved that he had asked this startling important question, about how he could be a better husband, that it took her several moments to respond. Finally, she gave him a list of three things. She wanted them to have a "date night" once a week; she wanted them each to have some "me" time alone one night a week (she wanted to take an art class, and was happy to have him play cards with his guy friends); and she wanted him to become a better kisser!

He promptly agreed to the first two. He admitted that he didn't know how to become a better kisser, but was very willing to take instruction. As hard as this was for him to admit, his vulnerability appealed to her. She was intrigued with his promise to follow all her instructions and not to get upset when she made suggestions. That night, the private lessons began! They were both turned on by her new role of "love instructor." The teacher/student role turned out to be a whole lot of fun for both of them, the spark was ignited, and their marriage was back on track!

It wasn't that all their problems were solved in one night, but their new closeness rebuilt their willingness to make things work with additional conversation. This shows how powerful that one simple action step was—asking Amy how he could be a better husband—and how it launched a positive process that rekindled the love that had brought them together a dozen years ago.

CHAPTER 10

Living Forward...
Committing to Your Life's Journey

As you improve your self-talk and begin to raise your self-esteem by carrying through on your commitments to new actions, you start to heal the feeling of being a victim of your life circumstances. As you claim your power of creativity, your orientation to everything shifts from the sense of being a victim of life to one of being a creative being who can make life express itself beautifully.

This new mindset helps you see life as an interactive and exciting process—one in which you are not constantly afraid of "what is going to happen next." Instead of allowing yourself to be overwhelmed by everyday developments, you feel more like your life is a potential creative tapestry.

This is where you begin to really recognize and reclaim your personal power and become the person you truly want to be. It is where you begin to believe in the possibility and probability of manifesting your dreams. It all starts with developing insight and understanding who you really are, what you really want, and what you're willing to do to become the person you want to be. Then you begin to make better choices. As you continue to carry out your action steps, you start seeing results that encourage you and build your trust in your ability to create the life you want.

Pay attention to what feels *truly right* to you and act in accordance with that feeling. If you say you are going to make a change, even if it is a very small one, make sure you stick with it, because keeping your word to yourself is what develops trust and a feeling of integrity and being right with yourself.

Having a fairly high match between what you say you are going to do and what you actually do builds self-integrity. It builds your will power to continue, because the results feel good and your level of self-love increases. Later in this chapter I will present a process to help you stay on track with your goals.

Your commitment to sticking with this process will be tested from time to time. In fact, obstacles along the path can almost be guaranteed. These are natural processes at work, not indications that you are weak or going in the wrong direction. The purpose of obstacles is to sharpen your commitment, energy, and focus on your goals and dreams. They are there to strengthen the muscle of your resolve, to cause you to work harder, or more clearly, or with more refined intention. Obstacles can prepare you by strengthening your resolve to get to the next level; thus they can be seen as motivators to help you to continue forward in achieving your goals. Obstacles can make you wiser and more focused, if you use your positive self-talk and affirmations to keep you on course.

In some cases your new choices may mean that you have to stand up or speak up for yourself and your new desires. It is important to stand up for your dreams. If you don't, who will?

Life Mastery is the Result of Good Choices

Life mastery comes from making good choices. Artful living is all about doing your best, such as the Japanese art of flower arranging, where every flower adds to the beauty of the design. Being very present for a simple task, without multi-tasking, can raise it to the level of an artful experience. Simple, focused actions lead to achieving results that can be as beautiful as a Japanese floral arrangement. Then those results will inspire you.

The secret to artful decisions is about making choices based on awareness of outcomes. That is why I am going to encourage you to visualize the desired outcome with intention, because it can feel daunting to contemplate the starting line of your goal. Obviously, you might feel overwhelmed as you think about the entire extent of your journey to the goal. To balance this sense of massive work ahead, you need the strong pull of the final outcome to motivate you to even start moving toward your goal.

This is something the grown-up brain can do. It is called critical thinking. It doesn't mean being judgmental. Critical thinking is the ability to be purposeful and reflective. It is the ability to see the difference between a good decision and a bad one based upon your values. Critical thinking helps you determine what to believe and what needs to be questioned. It helps you clarify goals and evaluate assumptions. It allows you to access your conclusions. With critical thinking you can accurately observe and interpret information with clarity and precision.

Critical thinking also helps you project outward. It makes you look at a forward outcome and the implications of all your decisions (and indecision!). If this feels like a big step, reduce it to smaller time segments. Critical thinking can be aided with questions such as: "What are the basic steps I need to take to accomplish this goal? How will I feel tomorrow if I take this action? What will happen if I do this? What will happen if I don't do this? How will these decisions affect the desired outcome?"

Remember, your decision making needs to be coming from positive self-talk. Otherwise, negative thinking can lead you down dead ends. Your communication skills need to come from the place of deserving good treatment from others, and the willingness to treat others with the same kindness with which you wish to be treated.

Life mastery is simply the consistency of making good choices. This is how you can benefit by increasing your critical thinking. It is an ongoing process. No one ever makes perfect decisions every time. If you stick with the commitment to keep making at least better choices than you made before, you will get there. Commitment is not a matter of doing good deeds for a week or two, then going back to old habits. You are going to have to cultivate patience with yourself, as you are a "work in progress." This kindness towards self needs to be coupled and balanced with the tenacity to continue to seek change and growth.

In time you will develop more confidence and trust in the process and the faith that you can make it happen. The irony of this is that you have to "act as if" you had confidence before you actually feel it. The confidence comes as a result of making changes; often it isn't present before. Just as with learning any new skill, such as playing the piano, you have to maintain a regimen of practice. It is going to take a lot of your energy focused in the direction of what you want in order to get you across your personal "finish line." Over time you will prove to yourself that you have the power to be the creative force in your life, and then the inspiration grows from there.

As you continue to see the alignment between your efforts and what is manifested in your life, it gets easier to change behaviors. Start to pay more attention to the connection between the actions you take and the results you get. Notice the impact of the large and small choices you make every day and how they are expressed in what you are manifesting. It is a tremendous gift to have this awareness, because it puts the reins of your life back in your own hands.

Hopefully you are now seeing how all the elements—positive self-talk, affirmations, believing in and using your creativity—work together to help you on your quest for a good and happy life. Start to pay more attention and put your focus on your strengths instead of giving so much attention to what is wrong or "weak" within you (in other words, stop believing your negative self-talk!). When you spend more time focusing on your strengths instead of your weaknesses, you are Living Forward!

Diana's Story

Diana was 56 when she came into therapy. Her primary issue was the lack of a significant other in her life. She longed for a lifelong partner, but felt she had "no room" for one. Her parents had divorced when she was twelve, after her father's messy affair, and had lived separately, three miles apart, ever since. Over the past year her father had been recovering from a stroke, and her mother from a broken hip. With both her siblings living abroad, Diana spent her evenings after work, going alternating to each parent's house, plus undertaking the occasional "emergency" baby sitting for her own two daughters, both of whom had toddlers.

Although she longed for companionship, it was clear she had, as she put it, no time and no room for a relationship. At first she couldn't even see what her first action step to address this issue might be. After some soul searching, she came up with a plan. She would ask her parents to move in together—in separate bedrooms—after having lived apart for forty-four years! They were still friendly, although they had fallen into the habit of speaking to each other through their children.

It took some doing, but her parents finally agreed to the move into a single dwelling. That gave Diana half the evenings of her life back, and she found that, with her parents now willing to help each other and to get some paid help, she was making only two visits a week, mostly to enjoy their company, instead of just constantly doing their chores.

Her second action step was to create a boundary with her daughters, as they tended to call her at the last minute for "emergency babysitting." She gathered her courage and told them that she was not going to be available for unscheduled babysitting. She let them know that she was willing to babysit on a regular schedule twice a month for each daughter, but didn't want to be the first one they called for the last-minute "drop everything" sitter. Her daughters started to work together, agreeing to help each other more often now that their mother had finally drawn a boundary line.

Now that she had created a little reliable space in her own life, Diana finally got brave enough to answer a personal ad posted through her church group. She met a nice man and, although they have been taking things very slowly, she felt for the first time in her adult life that she could make a date for Saturday night and know that she could keep it! Diana feels hopeful that, even if it doesn't work out with this man, she has created a space in her life for love.

CHAPTER

11

How Your Circle of Life Becomes a Spiral

Your Circle of Life is like a mandala, which is a spiritual image, often in the form of a circle, which represents completion or unity. It shows the interconnection between all the levels of life, and it is often mesmerizingly beautiful to see the intricate patterns of connectivity. Many people use making and gazing at mandalas as a form of meditation, healing, insight, stress relief, or problem solving. Your completed Circle of Life is your own personal mandala, and is as unique and perfect as you are!

Your Circle of Life mandala becomes the story of your life, both how it is in this moment and how it can unfold in the future. It is your personal mythic or hero's/heroine's journey, as it is a map of your choices, past, present, and future. It tells the story of where you are and where you are going, but it is also a tool or invitation to live life more fully. Using the six steps of the Circle of Life allows you to transform how your life and your mandala will play out.

According to Stanley Krippner, Ph.D., "Mandalas report wholeness, closure, and a completed journey. Mandalas are symbols or images to carry deeper meanings. Some examples are the Tibetan or Navajo sand mosaics or the monuments at Stonehenge."

One of my favorite books is *Mandala* by José Arguelles. Looking at the beautiful images in this book really inspired me, and I was amazed at the depth and meaning contained in those beautiful mandalas.

As you use the Circle of Life as a mandala or map to express the present, it can help you move forward. It can then become a life-long upward spiral. Over time you will see how your Circle of Life is a growing, changing, living map of your life. As you make changes, even tiny steps, your life and its expression through the circle will change to reflect your new experiences.

Keeping your circle current with your new changes helps remind you that nothing stays the same: your life is always moving and evolving. New choices open new directions, and everything begins to move in a positive flow. This new positivity empowers you to maintain wonderful momentum. Keep moving forward and continue to score and assess your own efficacy as you make these changes. By continuing to take the action steps that you are motivated to do you will learn how to progress in areas that are important to you, and you will feel that your life is moving in this more constructive and systematic way.

While we are aware that we need to make some changes in life, often we can lose focus, especially if we have multiple areas that we want to change at the same time. The Circle of Life can help you stay focused without getting frustrated or overwhelmed, because you can break progress down into simple action steps while keeping track of your development.

It helps to have a visual map or mandala so that you can see where you are, where you want to go, and what you need to do to get there.

Whether you do a new circle for special occasions, every year or every decade or during times in your life when you feel lost, you always have your first circle as a kind of continuum of your life with which you can reconnect. For example, maybe you have the same friends that you had as a teenager, or maybe you didn't have close friends as a teenager, but you do now. Seeing progress on the friend slice of your circle will anchor and inspire you. As you see large or small changes documented on your circle, it will delight you and motivate you to go farther in the same or a new direction.

Perhaps you have been wondering about a career or job change, and now you're willing to delineate this path into action steps. You can see how getting the healthy foundations of sleep, exercise, diet, supportive friends, and a significant other can give you the strength to move forward. It is fun to see how your circle gains positive scores with more pluses and checks as you make even small changes. This way you can see visible evidence of the changes and it gives you momentum. Now you become more willing to look at the areas in your life you scored as minuses. These are often neglected areas, which can be changed with a little bit of attention, using the processes in this book.

What began as your first basic circle then expanded to the outer circle. This became a map of completion for that specific phase of your life. Some people may choose to make a new circle because their outer circle has evolved so far beyond where they began that they need to start a new page.

One patient described how much her life had changed since she first started with her circle almost a year ago. She felt she was freed from the confines of the issues she had previously faced in her inner circle. She no longer felt the constraints that had her life "boxed in." When she came back to therapy, she announced that, not only did she feel liberated from how she had been living before, but felt free to contemplate her "new life" as she wanted to live it. Some people like building on their initial circle to always be able to see where they started. For them, the circle becomes an ongoing spiral, and the spiral then becomes a mandala or living map of their life.

Reviewing the Steps of the Circle of Life

To review, in the first phase of filling in the slices, you were looking only at the present, how things are in this moment. As you expanded to the outer ring of the circle, you were putting in what your intentions were for the future. This process can continue, creating a spiral of circles that evolve over time.

You can use your Circle of Life to move your vision into the future. This is the future as you would ideally like it to be. You write exactly what you would like your life to be like, including whatever changes you are willing to make. In other words, if all or most of our slices were pluses, how would that feel? What would your life be like? What would you be doing? How would you be living?

It is so important to exercise our imagination. It is where we fully let ourselves experience what our life would be like if we made some of these changes. Can you imagine life at this higher level? This is an important technique, because what you can imagine, you can begin to move toward.

You need to have a vision of what your life would look and feel like. This will help you to keep focused on where you want to go. Use your progressed Circle of Life as if it were a mandala guiding your life. Note how you would feel—as if these changes were already made. Like a spiritual muscle that gets stronger through use, this vision can be the fuel that gets you going and keeps you going. The image of a more perfect future is what gives you the juice to make the changes you need to make today. The more specific you are, the more you will frame a compelling image to move toward.

Use your Circle of Life as a process of continual fine-tuning. It is a mind-set that keeps you moving in the direction you want to go until your life is where you want it to be. It is helpful to have an image of where you see yourself being throughout your life.

Are there some goals, dreams, and aspirations that you have been putting on hold for numerous reasons? Perhaps there are some steps you could take that would move you in the direction of bringing passion and purpose into your daily life.

Lizzie's Story

For three years Lizzie had been going back and forth between two very different men. She had known Hal for eleven years, and he was stable, trustworthy, a good and dependable friend, and financially secure. Sexually Hal bored her and spiritually she felt there was no real connection. With Trevor, a member of an aspiring country-western band, she had a passionate love life, it was creatively stimulating, he made her laugh and they had great conversations, but he also had another girlfriend, whom he just wasn't going to give up.

Lizzie was almost 35 and feeling the ticking of the biological clock. Hal was willing to get married and have babies, although it was more for her than it was his true desire. Trevor did not want kids, but also didn't want to lose her, and called her "his muse." He said he still wanted her in his life, even if she was going to have kids with another man.

In order to help I suggested she make two circles, one for each relationship. When she did this and saw them side-by-side she was amazed to understand not only what each man brought, but what each man lacked. She had always seen positives and negatives in each relationship, but now seeing them all on paper and seeing some critical gaps in her basic needs made it all very clear.

The pressure to make a decision about her future was on her because Hal had a job offer in another city and she had to decide whether or not to move with him. After she took a hard look at both men with the new clarity that came from her creating a circle to picture each relationship, she realized that in both cases she was settling—and losing too much of what she really wanted.

It took some bravery to tell Hal she wasn't going to move across the country with him. It took even more bravery to tell Trevor that she no longer wanted to be his "second fiddle."

Lizzie realized that there was someone out there who would fill her slices in ways that didn't force her to choose among her core needs and desires. She felt sad losing them both, but excited that she was breaking a lifelong pattern of settling for other people's agendas and plans. She felt inspired to find Mr. Right, even if it meant for the first time in her life being alone for awhile.

Most importantly, she realized that she had been holding both men as her "last chance options," and she realized there really were better options out there for her; she just had to be willing to not settle for less than true happiness.

Part Three

∽

Using The Circle
of Life to Transform
Specific Areas of Your Life

CHAPTER

12

The Circle of Love—
The Couples Circle

The Couples Circle is a great way to get a relationship back on track. Many couples come into counseling to learn healthy relationship skills before they go to a deeper level of commitment, or sometimes as a last resort for keeping their relationship together. I have found the Couples Circle to be very helpful for those who want to make their relationship healthy and successful.

When you make a Couples Circle, you have a choice. You can either do each person's complete circle and view them side-by-side, or you can put all the information for both partners in the same circle. In this case, you just divide the slices in half. I use two different colored pens, one color for each partner. Seeing the information side-by-side is very illuminating. It may take longer to complete a Couples Circle, but it is well worth the time.

As you begin to see the flow of each other's lives—or areas that are empty—this will initiate a healthier objective

Dual Couples Circle of Life

Name _____

Date _____

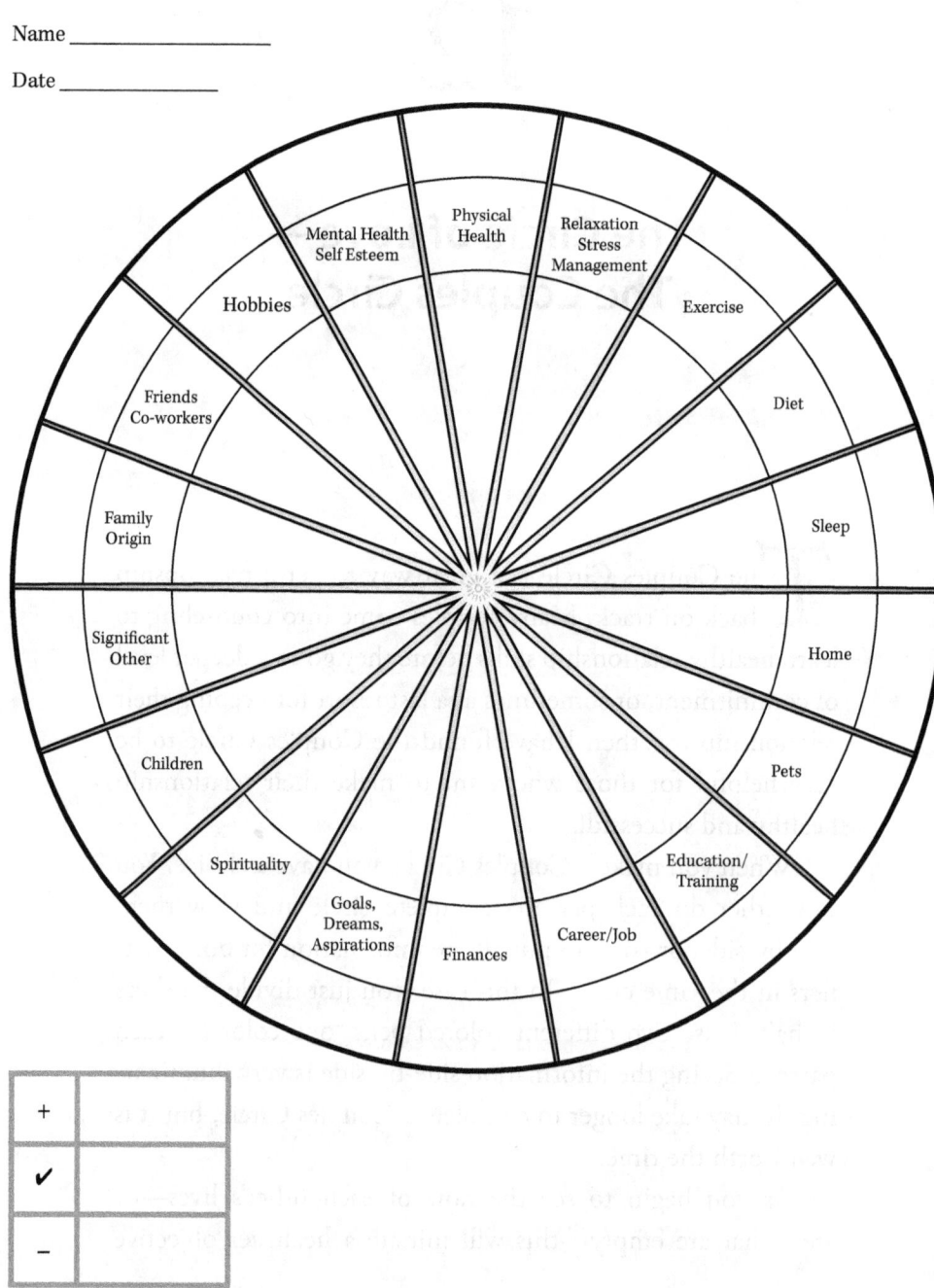

+	
✓	
−	

Name _____

Date _____

Wheel sections (clockwise from top):
- Physical Health
- Relaxation Stress Management
- Exercise
- Diet
- Sleep
- Home
- Pets
- Education/Training
- Career/Job
- Finances
- Goals, Dreams, Aspirations
- Spirituality
- Children
- Significant Other
- Family Origin
- Friends Co-workers
- Hobbies
- Mental Health Self Esteem

+	
✔	
−	

Couples Circle of Life

Name _____   Name _____

Date _____   Date _____

- Physical Health
- Mental Health / Self Esteem
- Hobbies
- Friends / Co-workers
- Family Origin
- Significant other
- Children
- Spirituality
- Goals, Dreams, Aspirations
- Finances
- Career/Job
- Education/Training
- Pets
- Home
- Sleep
- Diet
- Exercise
- Relaxation / Stress Management

+	
✔	
−	

+	
✔	
−	

conversation about what is working or not working, and how these factors influence your partnership. You will see both your strengths as individuals and also areas where you could each improve. As you look at your own circle, you will see how imbalances may be affecting the partnership.

Here are some examples from couples who have greatly benefited by doing the Couples Circle process.

Bev and Kyle

When Bev and Kyle came into counseling, they were on the verge of breaking up. They couldn't even imagine the possibility of getting their relationship back on track. They were arguing all the time, the dogs were sleeping between them, and they hadn't been intimate in eight months.

Bev, who was very task-oriented, had a long list of things that she felt Kyle should be doing. She was constantly disappointed in him because he wasn't doing the things on her list. On his side, he was tired of being nagged, and, although he often appeared to give in to her requests, he didn't really want to do what he kept saying he would do—which he said just to please her—so he ended up not completing these tasks.

When we did the Couples Circle together, one thing became immediately apparent. Kyle had given up his hobbies in order to have time for Bev. He stopped playing softball with his friends, a game that had been going on since their high school days. He also stopped going to his weekly poker game. Kyle was a superb poker player, and this evening had been a high point of his week.

Bev had asked him to stop both these activities, because she needed more help with the fixer-upper house they had bought together that she wanted to re-sell. Kyle wasn't even conscious of how angry he was about having given up these two important areas of his recreational life. He was unconsciously taking it out on her by not finishing home repair projects.

Once they both realized this, Bev immediately said she would rather have him take some time for himself and return to those two activities that brought him so much pleasure. He felt guilty because she had funded the down payment on the house and he didn't feel he was pulling his weight. That was why he hadn't brought up the subject of wanting to return to his favorite activities. This silence took a toll on his mental health because he needed this outlet.

As we began to formulate simple action steps, Bev and Kyle began to see the possibility that they could get their relationship back on track. As soon as Kyle realized that he needed to speak up and not just agree when he didn't mean it—although it upset the status quo for a few weeks—Bev actually began to respect him more. This led to their attraction to each other being rekindled. Kyle felt happier, knowing that his two favorite activities were back on his schedule again. He enjoyed seeing his buddies, and he remembered how important this time was to him. His resentment level dropped. Now that he knew he only had to agree to the projects he was really willing to do, he began to complete them.

Bev admitted that this was working much better, because at least she felt she knew what she could count on Kyle doing and what she would have to hire contractors to do. She realized this was the most frustrating part of how they had been interacting in the past, because she was always disappointed while waiting and looking at unfinished projects, not knowing whether they would ever get done. She was grateful for the excellent work that Kyle did, and understood that she needed him to set his own timetable for completion.

After three months of this new plan, both their resentment levels had dropped, and they felt inspired and hopeful about their future together.

Malia and Devon

Malia and Devon had been married for seven years when they came into therapy. Both entrepreneurs, they often worked seven days a week. Even if it was just a meeting with a client, there never seemed to be a day when they both had the entire day off. Every time they made plans together for just the two of them, one or the other had a "client emergency." They weren't actively fighting, but they hadn't made love in three years. They felt they had no common goals and were living like roommates. They both loved the house they lived in and all the furnishings. As Malia put it, "I feel like we are staying together for the house!"

When we did their Couples Circle, we realized that there were some small changes that could make a big difference in their relationship. Here were the steps they agreed upon. The first rule they made was, "No TV on during dinner." Second, they would make one sunset date each week and take a walk on the beach. They would both put the sunset walk in their planners and treat it as if it was a client meeting that couldn't be cancelled. They agreed to go to a Sunday morning yoga class they both enjoyed and then have brunch afterwards.

Next they agreed to take three minutes each before going to bed, sharing and listening to each other about what had happened in each other's day. Finally, they agreed to a five-minute cuddling and make-out session two times a week before going to sleep, with no sense of obligation for sex; at the same time, no matter how tired they felt, they both knew they could connect in this playful way. It wasn't long before they began having sex twice a week, which they hadn't done since their first year together.

Malia and Devon learned that even small changes—ones that they could *both agree on*—could lead to big changes. When I saw them three months later, they were doing better than ever, and they laughed about how bad things used to be between them.

Darlene and Don's Story

Darlene and Don had been married for seventeen years. When they came in for counseling, they didn't seem to have any idea of what was going on in each other's busy schedules—so it was no wonder they couldn't connect or find any time to spend together. They only made love a couple of times a year, and they could barely even manage to share a meal, a movie, or a moment together without squabbling so much that neither one wanted to be near the other.

They had completely different perceptions about why they couldn't get in sync with each other. After they both did their circles and compared them side by side, it became clear that so many "impossibilities" were actually based on a lack of communication.

I had Don and Darlene start by reading John Gray's wonderful book, *What You Feel You Can Heal*. This practical and insightful book has been invaluable to many of my patients. Reading it, they began to understand the consequences of not communicating with each other about the issues that bothered them.

The damage that comes from not telling the truth, or even resorting to white lies, saying things like "I'm fine" when that was far from the case, results not just in withholding information, but ultimately in withholding love. It can lead to a feeling of resentment that is so uncomfortable that you start to feel yourself beginning to reject or pull away from your partner. You begin to question whether or not you want to be together.

If you are not dealing with these conflicted feelings, they can lead to emotionally shutting down. Instead of clearing the air by expressing your thoughts and feelings, you begin to keep quiet, perhaps just to keep the peace. You lose your enthusiasm and aliveness. Before you know it, you can barely feel the love you once felt for your partner. This is a dangerous situation if not addressed. In a relationship, when the truth is not being shared, soon the love begins to be polluted by this stored-up energy. Soon the magic that was once there is buried under the load of negative emotions.

Next, one or both partners start to feel a creeping numbness. Once you disconnect from your feelings, there is a loss of ability to feel negative as well as positive emotions. The consequence of suppressing one emotion is that the others, even the positive ones, get buried at the same time. The result is a loss of the feelings of joy, passion, and love.

This is exactly what Don and Darlene discovered had happened to them. They began the journey back to healthier communication by addressing small issues at first. As they resolved issues in small steps, they built back the trust in the love that had brought them together.

When they came into therapy, even deciding on a restaurant they both felt like going to resulted in so much arguing and miscommunication that neither one ended up feeling like a night out. In ten minutes they went from resistance to each other's ideas to resentment about having to "settle" for the other person's choice, to rejecting each other's suggestions, to not wanting even to share a meal together. The solution was to make a list of "pre-approved" restaurants that they both liked. There were only three of them—but they both agreed that any of the three were acceptable. When there was an opportunity for a night out, they just went down the list, going to the first one, then the second, and so on, and then they would repeat the list. As simple as it sounds, it took all the negotiation out of the process. It worked well for about six months, when they both agreed to try a new place; that became fun also, and got added to the list. One year later, they have seven approved restaurants, and the plan still works.

Another area that had been a source of stress was eating dinner at home in front of the TV. He liked to replay sports or news during dinner, and she liked to replay the dance shows. It seemed that whatever one wanted to watch bothered the other. Either way, one of them was unhappy, so they finally agreed to no TV during home meals. Both agreed that the lack of TV was worth the lack of arguments! Now they were starting to talk to each other during dinner.

Next was making a once-a-week date for sex. They alternated, that is, one week he would do anything she wanted to do (even if it was just ten minutes for a back rub), and the next week, she would do anything he wanted to do. They didn't think this plan would work at all at first, but it broke the ice of not having intimacy, and after awhile, as they developed trust in each one's desire to bring pleasure to the other, it began to revive their sex life.

Within a few months they were having "off-schedule" sex, which had the added benefit of being spontaneous and fun!

This new passion ignited only after several months of "sex-by-schedule."

Although this routine seemed a little forced at first, it revived their connection, and they both felt much better about themselves and the marriage with this new plan in play. They felt inspired that, if they could handle this seemingly impossible issue, they could handle anything with good and open communication.

Telling the Truth Restores the Magic

When the whole truth hasn't been shared in a while, it is like not taking out the trash for a long period of time. It starts with creating a small problem, and then it can become an unpleasant situation if left unhandled. In a relationship, when the truth is not being shared, the love begins to erode because of the stored-up negative energy. Then the magic that was once there is buried under the load of negative emotions.

Next, one or both partners start to shut down. Once this numbness overtakes them, there is a loss of ability to feel positive emotions as well as negative ones. As we have seen, the price of suppressing your emotions is that even the good ones get buried. The result is a loss of the feelings of joy, passion, and love.

The good news is, if positive emotions were there once, they can usually be renewed. Just as you can take out the trash and get the room cleaned, with diligence you can take out the emotional trash and rediscover positive feelings.

To help you recognize the consequences of not telling the truth and communicating what you are feeling, in his book *What You Can Feel You Can Heal*, Dr. John Gray talks about the four warning signs, the Four Rs that eat away at happiness if you stop telling your partner the truth. The Four Rs are resistance, resentment, rejection, and repression. (See Gray's Chapter Five, "What Happens When You Don't Tell the Truth.")

The first sign that you are not speaking up is a lingering feeling of resistance. You start to resist what your partner is saying or doing or requesting. You begin to retreat into your shell. When this resistance takes over, it is time to look inside and see what you are feeling and find a healthy way to express it.

If you ignore the resistance, it can lead to getting irritated over small things that your partner is doing. They become very large in your mind, bothering you more every time you allow yourself to focus on these behaviors. This leads to feeling resentment, which could be followed by rejection of your partner.

Instead of clearing the air by expressing your thoughts and feelings, if you decide to keep quiet, perhaps just to keep the peace, this can move you into a state of numbness. You lose your enthusiasm and aliveness. Before you know it, you can barely feel the love you once felt for your partner.

CHAPTER

13

The Importance of Self-Care

Self-care is one the most important skills to develop to have a healthier life. Sometimes people sense that their lives are out of balance; they know they need to make changes, and they assume these changes are going to be very big and dramatic. You may indeed need to make some big changes, but often I start by having patients look at how they are doing with something as simple as the four fundamental self-care aspects—the quality of their sleep, nutrition, exercise, and relaxation. These areas of our life are basic, and they are the foundation upon which everything else will work or not. Ironically, it is often these areas that busy people may overlook when they are seeking to change the quality of their life.

One good way to start to change your life is to look at these basic needs of self-care. Focusing on these aspects restores the sense of control over your own life and the quality of your experience. If you are feeling that your life is out of control, it is guaranteed that one or more of the four self-care aspects are out of balance. As you make self-care a priority, you begin to make better choices, and this quickly expands to rapid improvement in other areas of your life.

The Four Main Self-Care Areas

1. Sleep

Numerous studies show that sleep deprivation (in terms of duration) or quality of sleep (in terms of slower, deeper brain wave states) will result in emotional distress, lack of productivity, and loss of concentration. The bottom line is, if you are not getting enough sound sleep, you will find it hard to function at your best on a long- term basis.

2. Nutrition

You've heard the expression, "You are what you eat." Food is the basic fuel that our body needs for energy and vitality. If you are putting garbage in, you will get garbage out in terms of your energy level. Lack of energy will affect your motivation to move forward in your life. Even if you are not ready to make massive changes in how you eat, identifying perhaps one or more specific habits that you are willing to change will have a major impact on your body.

For example, when one of my patients, Ron, was doing his Circle of Life, he noticed that he was having three caffeine sodas a day, one at lunch, one at three PM, and one at dinner. He chose to reduce his soda intake to one a day at three PM, having water instead of the other two sodas. He found he really enjoyed his afternoon treat more than when he was having one with almost every meal. He lost two pounds that first month, which encouraged him to look at other eating habits that he could modify without feeling deprived. Within three months he had lost ten pounds without feeling that he was dieting.

3. Exercise

Chances are you are aware of how important exercise is for well-being. In addition to the importance of fitness for best functioning in every area of your life, exercise strengthens the immune system, improves mood, and enhances libido. As you regain control over your weight, your sense of self-esteem rises. If the form of exercise you do is fun for you, you get added benefits. Regular cardio exercise three to five times a week raises the heart rate, helps circulation, and tones or enhances just about every bodily function.

4. Relaxation and Stress Management

Relaxation renews our energy. It is essential to balance "doing" with "being" by using a relaxation practice. There are as many ways to relax as there are people, and what works for one person may be a total chore for another. Many people find that meditation is a perfect way to relax. For others this may be too challenging. There are many relaxation techniques and many forms of meditation. You will benefit from any activity that helps you manage stress, such as exercises that increase breathing capacity, endorphin release, blood flow to muscles, and a myriad of other physical and mental benefits.

I love to hear how different people find stress-relieving benefits through various activities such as golf, sports, fishing, reading, gardening, cooking, creating art, listening to music, playing chess, dancing, walking, or doing improv comedy, yoga, or tai chi. As long as it works for you, it is the right method!

When clients come in to work on their Circle of Life and I ask them how they are doing with their relaxation and stress management slice, if they tell me they have no time to relax, I know we have to make that a priority. Without relaxation and stress management methods in your life to balance productive activity, it is a short trip to burnout. For patients who say they don't even know what relaxes them, our first step is to find one or two activities that create this effect. It is smart to have more than one activity, so that your relaxation is not controlled by weather conditions, teammates, or other external circumstances, and to have at least one activity that you can do on your own.

Making sure that these four elements of self-care are working well is really the foundation of wellbeing in every area of your life. Without even one of these four functioning as strong pillars in your life, you will find you have diminished enthusiasm, focus, and energy for making the best decisions and for working effectively and productively. When you don't have the right fuel, your energy diminishes, and you will not feel that you have the gumption to move toward your purpose.

Also, if one or more of these self-care elements are out of balance, it is an indicator that you are over-committed in other areas of your life. You then begin to feel like a hamster in a cage, running on a wheel, exhausted, and not getting anywhere you want to go.

Once you remind yourself how important these foundation elements are to support other aspects of your life, you will be willing to prioritize these important pillars of wellness. So often we give up aspects of these essentials because of commitments to other people or other agendas, and the price of this is imbalance and distress in all other areas of our body and mind.

Returning to a commitment to self-care helps us focus and maintain optimal functioning in all areas. These are the essential ingredients for a happy and healthy life.

Randy's Story: Finding Relaxation

Randy was a hard-working attorney, age 46 and single. When he did his Circle of Life, his relaxation slice was empty. He couldn't even remember the last time he had consciously done something to relax. I gave him homework to make a list of things that he had done in his younger life that relaxed him. Although he had put effort into trying to come up with this list, he came back the next week with a blank page.

To spark his imagination, I asked him what he recorded on TV, and discovered that he taped the reality dance shows. Since he had never taken a lesson and couldn't dance, he didn't consider this a possibility for himself. He said his favorite dance to watch was the rumba.

His stress management homework for the next week was to set up a private lesson with a dance teacher. He found a teacher who made "house calls" or, in his case, office calls, and he began lessons instead of lunch on Tuesdays. It wasn't easy at first, and he had to take some teasing from his associates. Randy's teacher noticed that he had a natural ability, and told him about a female student, Sophia, who was looking for a rumba dance partner for an amateur competition. He said No at first, but finally agreed to meet Sophia for one lesson. It turned out to be so much fun that he agreed to be her partner in the amateur competition which was in four months. He and Sophia took second place, and the best part was that they began dating! So following his bliss in one area opened up gifts beyond his wildest dreams.

Constance's Story: Finding Relaxation

Constance referred to herself as "the poster child for the Type A personality." She lived in a house with her parents, her husband, and their three children. She ran her own internet business, took care of the house and her parents, cooked all the meals, and felt like all she did was take care of everything and everyone else. Her oldest daughter felt that Constance was always meddling in her life and telling her what to do; her husband felt neglected; and the only time she felt any peace was the fifteen minutes a day when she took her dog for a morning walk. "I realized I've started talking to the dog," she said. "I tell him all my woes."

In her Circle of Life, Constance had nine minuses, but she decided to focus her attention on just one minus area—and that was relaxation. Although there were several areas of her life that were "big minuses," she didn't feel she could add anything more into her world. "If I even added fifteen minutes anywhere, it would cause chaos somewhere else."

Her action plan didn't involve adding anything. Her need was to eliminate something. Her goal was to free up three hours a week by not doing anything for anybody else for three hours! Her plan was to turn one night a week into "Pizza and Jacuzzi Night," which was one night when she didn't have to cook. She informed her family of what she would be doing on Tuesday nights and invited them all to participate. They had put in a Jacuzzi for her parents, but they had stopped using it.

At first her kids viewed this tub as "rehab" for their parents and weren't interested, but they decided to give it a try, as did her husband. She found it brought them all together, and, without being busy cooking and serving, she was able to focus on listening to the details of her family's lives. It turned into a great bonding time, because she was finally able to give her full attention to what they had to say.

Then she decided to make some more "me time." She had always wanted to take a Jazzercise class, which was at the community center around the corner, and she decided to invite her husband. To her shock, he agreed to come! After all, he had gained a few pounds too. There were only two men in the class; one was in his seventies, and the other was her husband.

As they kept up with the class and made some dietary changes, he lost fifteen pounds and she lost eight; her new body size enabled her to wear some of her favorite clothes again. A side benefit of the class was that she began to notice the other women checking her husband out. Many women told her how lucky she was to have a husband who was willing to come to a class like this. She began to feel more grateful for his loyal and playful spirit, and the twinge of jealousy was surprisingly useful! Seeing the women's focus on her husband made her pay attention to him in ways that she hadn't done in a long time.

They hadn't had physical intimacy in many years, and now they began having "make-out" sessions after dance class— sweaty T-shirts and all! It was so much fun that he suggested they take class three times a week. Constance had an even more fun idea: like Randy, she had always wanted to take ballroom dance lessons. Constance wanted to plan to go on a cruise and dance. That would be their first vacation together in seven years.

Her husband beamed. "I just like to see you happy," he said. Constance realized how lucky she really was to have a husband who was so easy to please!

CHAPTER 14

Creating Passion, Purpose, and Direction

In Part One of this book, your circle was focusing on what is happening in this present moment in your life in the various areas you wish to explore. In this section of the book, we are looking forward. This is where you examine what is important to you and begin to design a life based on your goals and dreams and what you would like to accomplish. Here is where you look at what you need to do to move in the direction of your goals.

Bring in your critical thinking skills to help you chart your course. As you look at your completed Circle of Life, you'll want to see how all the parts interrelate. Notice that your life is the sum total of the choices you have made and are making. The choices you made in the past got you where you are today. This is not about judging yourself. At this point in the process it is important to notice that certain choices lead to certain results. If you are not happy with these results, you need to make different choices and take different actions.

As simple as it sounds, it is true. The same choices will cause the same results. Different choices bring different results. To get to some place different, you will need to take small but important steps in a new direction. It will come down to priorities. Noticing how things are right now is how you begin to change them for the future. The sooner you recognize the need for change, the more capable you are of making the changes you want, as long as you don't expect everything to change overnight.

As with all behavioral changes in the Circle of Life, start with a reasonable, sensible change that moves you a little bit forward toward where you want to go. In time, small changes lead to bigger ones. Soon you are in no doubt that you will manifest everything you set your mind to!

Often people come into therapy feeling they have lost their zest or reason for living. Many people struggle with this issue and this feeling of losing one's way can happen at any age or stage of life. People who are facing this kind of crisis are often focused on the past and past relationships and disappointments, feeling little or no hope for the future. Therapy can help get them reconnected with their purpose and passion.

If finding your passion, purpose, and direction is an issue for you, it is important to know that there is light at the end of the tunnel. As soon as you get yourself redirected towards what you feel passionate about, your life begins to turn around. This does not have to be a long and arduous process. If you have totally lost your way, be patient, because it may take some time. It gets easier as soon as you start steering in the right direction. By "right" direction, I don't mean in a moral sense, but in the sense of what feels "right" to you.

Here are some tips to help you find your way. Start by making a list or taking stock of your strengths as a person. Take some time with this process. Don't just accept the first answers that come to mind. When I asked my patient, David, who worked in the insurance business, what his strengths were, he answered quickly, "I don't have any important strengths." I sent him home to think about it. A week later he came in with a short but important list: "I care about people, I am honest, I appreciate beauty, I can build simple websites, I love finding great photos and images online."

David wasn't very impressed with his short list. As we talked about it more, he realized he totally enjoyed himself when he built a website for his neighbor, which he did for free. His neighbor was very appreciative, encouraging David to think about doing it for others for a reasonable fee. David began to take stock and really own the things he did well and enjoyed doing. Within a month he had two paying website clients, and he decided to take a class to learn more sophisticated skills.

Claim Your Strengths—They are Clues to Your Happiness

We all have strengths. We just don't always acknowledge them. The sooner you can own and tap into your personal strengths, the sooner you can put them to use. The importance of your list of strengths is that it will lead you to focus on what brings you joy and happiness.

Also, when you start using and applying your strengths, you feel happier. It is depressing to feel that you are not using your strengths in life, so, if you don't feel that you get to use them in your job or daily life, you can find ways to use them in your hobbies, or in volunteer work, or by helping friends—whatever it takes to kick-start your confidence. Getting this energy moving will lift your spirits.

You will be surprised how quickly switching your focus from what is wrong with you, or what is lacking in your life, to what is good and right, and fun and effective, will begin to create significant changes. Remember that you get more of what you focus on. So focus on the things you love, the things that bring a smile to your face, and let them be your beacon. Instead of navigating from a long list of "shoulds" and "should nots" and endless "To Do" lists, focus on what brings you joy.

If you are a highly intelligent and disciplined person, at first this may feel as if you are goofing off or being unrealistic. Trust the process. Trust that, if you are excited by something, it is a clue to its rightness for you. You may have to work with it to find its right form. It may need to evolve over time until you can discover more about yourself, especially if it hasn't been out and dusted for a while. For now, all we are looking for are clues to what is your truest expression. We have to get out from under the laundry list of your everyday responsibilities in order to find this gem of inspiration!

It is there. Trust me. You just have to be willing to look.

Valuing your own skills and strengths will reignite your enthusiasm and satisfaction. For more resources, visit a website called Authentic Happiness (www.authentichappiness.org), which has a series of questionnaires that researchers in the field of positive psychology have contributed to help individuals find their signature strengths, assess their level of happiness and meaning in life, and uncover many other positive perspectives to help them more deeply understand themselves.

Goals, Dreams, and Aspirations: Making a Joyful "To Do" List

No matter what age you are when you are reading this book, it is never too early or too late to consider doing the things that bring you true joy. Make a list of things, big and small, that would or do bring you joy. What are the things you have always wanted to do but have perhaps put off for various reasons? Are there some pursuits or activities that you have put on the back burner?

Could you put some of these joyful activities back in your life, even in some small ways, right now? In the same way we did with other areas of your life where you wanted to make changes, sometimes just putting your toe in the water, in the direction of your goals, dreams, or aspirations, can put you where you should be.

One of my patients, who was seventy-six, decided to take golfing lessons. He had played well as a young man, but quit in his thirties because he had family responsibilities. He hadn't held a club in forty-five years when he met up with his instructor, who was forty years younger than he. In his own words, it "wasn't pretty at first." Within six months, however, younger golfers were starting to follow him around, buy him drinks, and pick his brain for tips on how to improve their swing. This brought him almost as much joy as his game. At the age of seventy-eight, he started giving lessons, because he got "tired of people picking his brain for free."

Another patient was in her mid-fifties when she decided to complete her Ph.D. It is never too late to follow up on a dream!

Put these dreams on paper on your Circle of Life in the slice for goals, dreams, and aspirations. Whether there is one item, a handful, or a long list, it will act like a compass and help you point your footsteps onto the path. Having conscious awareness of your heart's desires adds a sense of meaning and satisfaction and becomes a guiding light. Remember that you don't have to make huge steps, just conscious steps.

Maybe you always had a dream of living in France. Putting it on paper will help give the vision momentum. You might just pay attention when a house trade for the summer in Provence is listed in an advertisement. You might just start by taking French lessons and meet a buddy who might be willing to be a travel companion on a month-long trip.

In other words, the specific details of the dream may be a work in progress, but taking steps toward it will make your life feel more on track. It will draw potential new opportunities that move you in the right direction. Once you have reminded yourself of the things that bring you joy and added them to this slice, you can begin taking steps toward a more wonderful life today and creating an upward spiral momentum to a joyful life for the future!

Stevie's Story

Stevie was nineteen when he dropped out of an expensive Ivy League school and returned home, because he just didn't feel he could handle the pressure of life at college. At home he was still having trouble sleeping, was awake until three or four AM, and then was getting up at two in the afternoon. He was barely eating, unless his mother made meals for him. He was depressed, feeling that he was a total loser. He wasn't exercising at all, except to take his dogs to the beach.

When he did his Circle of Life, the only thing that he felt was working was his relationship with his cat and two dogs. He liked drawing cartoons of them and coming up with clever captions, but he called that just "useless doodling."

The only thing that even made him smile was shooting videos of his dogs, which had learned to boogey-board with him! He couldn't even imagine applying for work (much less working, even if he did get hired). His parents were at their wits' end, which made him feel even more a failure.

When I asked him if he could think of one small action step, he toyed with the idea of film school, but it was expensive, and he didn't think he could handle the competitiveness described on the college's student blogs.

Finally, he had a breakthrough, when one of the videos of his animals that he shot and edited to a music track and posted on You-Tube got him a request for "a funny musical video of my dog" from someone a few miles away. Stevie charged $50 for the two-minute video, but it was worth a million bucks in inspiration. The friend showed the video to *his* friends, and Stevie immediately got two more paying clients. He clearly had a talent for filming and editing, as well as working with animals on camera.

Stevie made his own website, and began putting up fliers letting people know about his unique service. Starting with recognizing what he loved and what he was good at, even though it didn't seem like much at the time, began a positive process of reclaiming his life. Two months later, he had nine clients and nine hilarious, very clever dog videos on his website. He raised his rate to $75! He was able to buy himself some new shoes that he wanted, instead of wearing the old ones he had been wearing for two years because he didn't want to ask his parents for anything more. The best news was how he was feeling about himself.

Meeting and interacting with clients started him sleeping on a fairly normal schedule, which had the added benefit of his being able to get up for early morning surfing. Two of his clients preferred lunchtime meetings, and with his healthier sleep and exercise routine his appetite returned. He was feeling better physically and mentally. "I feel normalized," as he put it, and he began to feel inspired about his future. His parents are behind him 100% and are helping him to create a business plan to take his venture to the next level.

CHAPTER 15

Teen Circles—What's My Life All About?

Whoever said that the teenage years were "The Time of Your Life" probably doesn't have a very good memory. For some teens, it is a fun and adventurous time. For most, it is a fairly challenging life passage. There are so many stressors that can derail even the happiest teen. The good news is that it can be easier to navigate these years with some help from the Circle of Life process.

For teens, doing their own Circle of Life can be a tool to help them feel a greater sense of control over their life. Building this habit early can give them a foundation that will serve them all their lives. It can be really useful to have objectives to help them make progress in areas that are important to them. As long as they are interested or willing to do the process, it is never too soon to start.

Although the issues and slices of a teen circle might be simplified, the circle itself is just as powerful. Teens should pick the slices that are relevant to their personal lives. Some of the slices I've seen teens use focus on their love life, their friends, school, work, family relationships, sense of self, and body image. As with the adult circle, they should start with the basics of self-care: sleep, food, exercise, and relaxation.

Sleep, in particular, is so important to being able to handle stress effectively; with the overuse of cell phones and texting, it is alarming how many teens are totally sleep- deprived. Recent research has also indicated that school starts much too early for the average teen body.

If you are the parent of teenagers, you can invite them to make their own Circle of Life, either on their own, or with a friend, or even with you. Let them tell you how they want to do it. It is great if they want to do it on their own, because they will really be truthful and get a lot out of the process. If they choose to do it with you, it can be a wonderful bonding process. Make sure they are putting in their own answers, not the ones they think you want to hear.

Here are some stories from teens who really benefited from doing their first Circle of Life.

Leilani's Story

"Doing my Circle of Life really helped me, because I was feeling like time was going by so fast, and I really needed to do my college applications. It helped me to realize I needed to put some time into that. Once I got that clear in my brain and made a list of all the deadlines, I could decide which ones to do first. I am really proud of myself because I got all of them, except one, done in time. Then I felt I could really enjoy my Christmas holiday, because I knew I had done what I needed to do."

Keoki's Story

"I didn't think I would like doing the Circle of Life at first, but I got into it. I really wanted a car. I had saved about $600 from my job. Doing the circle thing gave me a way of thinking about how much I needed to save and for how long. I just put it all on paper. I needed to save $35 a week. If I put that aside, I could spend the rest of the money on other stuff I wanted. It gave me a plan, and I stuck to it all but one week when I needed some new clothes. I felt really proud of myself that in seven months I had enough for a used car that my neighbor was selling."

Trisha's Story

"Until I did my first Circle of Life, it never occurred to me that I never do anything to relax. Like my parents, I am sort of a driven person. I can't help it. I realized I was getting totally burned out in my junior year. I have a part-time job and so every minute was accounted for. I wasn't doing anything fun. I had stopped going to ballet class and I really missed it. I realized I could take a half an hour each day to just do the basic ballet barre exercises in my room before I do homework. Then I started taking a class on Saturday at the Y, even though it was more of a beginner class. I liked it because there was no pressure, so it gave my brain a recharge. I didn't even realize I was so burned out. I am surprised that, even though I am taking more time out for myself, I am getting more done. I never would have believed that."

Allie's Story

"I didn't realize it until I did my Circle of Life, but I was trying to juggle three groups of friends. One group was from my old grade school, one group was from my current school, and one group was from my photography club. I was spending so much effort trying to give everyone equal time, and it was driving me crazy. When I did my Circle of Life, I saw how much time this was taking up, and I didn't really like spending all that much time every week. I decided to have "mini-reunions" twice a year with my old friends, and not try to keep up with texting them every day. I also realized that my new friends in the photography club were the ones most important to me, and I stopped trying to please everyone. I am a lot happier now."

Hank's Story

"My girlfriend and I broke up, because I did something really stupid. I got drunk at a party and had sex with a friend of hers. That's when I lost all my friends, because we had all the same friends. It was like they all just ganged up on me. I know what I did was wrong, and I wish I never did it. I couldn't get anyone to hear my side of the story. I can't believe how cruel people can be. When I did my Circle of Life, I was able to start focusing on what was really important to me. I stopped chasing them. It still hurt my feelings, but after about a month, one or two friends started talking to me again. I realized the difference between real friends and those who just follow the leader. Then this girl in class that I never really paid attention to asked me out. She's very different from the type of girl I normally date, but I like her. She's very honest and real. I think I kind of like her more than I thought I would."

Marnie's Story

"I liked choosing what slices I wanted in my circle. It really made me see what was really important to me, and what I could eliminate. Kind of like cleaning up your room, except it is like cleaning up your life. I know it is just on paper, but it makes you think differently about stuff. Then you choose what you really want to spend time doing. It's funny, but at first I didn't want to go to the next step where you put the checks and minuses, because I felt like, 'Well, if I fix my whole life now, and I'm only fourteen, will there be anything left to do if everything is perfect?' Then I understood that this is a process you use your whole life. There's always a new level of opportunity to make your world even better."

Chaz's Story

"At first I was like, whoa! I didn't realize there were so many areas of my life to balance out. It was kind of overwhelming when I first looked at it. Then I saw, there are some areas that are good, and some not so good, and some that suck. So I just have to start making more of them good, or great. Because that's how I want to live my life anyway. I'm glad I started this. I already feel better about how my life is."

Becka's Story

"My mother was always nagging me about my weight. I was 27 pounds heavier than my skinny friends. They all weighed within seven pounds of each other. I think they liked having a fat girl around because it made them feel skinnier! I just didn't feel like I could do anything about it. I didn't want to be the only one on a diet around my friends. So when I did my Circle, what I decided was I would eat a really healthy breakfast at home instead of eating fast food. Dinner would be healthy too, and I was not going to have dessert or soda at dinner. Then at lunch or with my friends, I could have whatever I wanted, so I wouldn't feel cheated because they were having it and I couldn't. This was good, because I didn't feel like I was really being deprived, because I could have whatever I wanted when I was eating with them. Even these small changes were a big deal, because I lost three pounds the first month. Then I decided to give up soda and fruit juice for a year. Just drink water. I thought I would hate it. The truth is, I feel better. I'm not so sleepy in the afternoon. Now I am starting to really learn about healthy food and things. My plan is to lose the 27 pounds in a year. I don't have to feel like I am on a diet."

Paul's Story

"I never really thought about how important sleep was until I started doing the Circle of Life process and I had to really look at how many hours of sleep I was getting. Between homework, texting, and working on my band's website, I was falling asleep at around 3 A.M. and getting up at 7:30 A.M. for school. I had just been doing that for so long, I didn't even think about it. I would doze in my morning classes and sleep at lunch, so then

I would pig out after school. I would study hard, and then the next day, I would forget, like, half of what I was studying, and I didn't put it together that this was all about not sleeping enough. I decided to just try it as an experiment, because I didn't really believe it at first, but I forced myself to go to bed at midnight. Since I knew I had to get everything done, I had to eliminate lying on the couch and watching TV except on weekends, when I catch up with my recorded shows. I couldn't believe it, but getting more sleep was really amazing. I felt better. I was doing better in gym class and all my classes, because first of all I was awake, but also I could remember more stuff. I was up in time for breakfast, so that helped too, and my skin got better. I had more patience with my younger brother and with my girlfriend too. I wasn't on such a short fuse. I just can't believe how important getting enough sleep is. I'm telling all my friends how different I feel and letting them know I'm not going to be texting them as much. They didn't believe me at first that getting enough sleep could make such a difference in every area of your life, but now they say I look like a new person."

Jessica's Story

"When I moved here from Michigan, I lost all my friends. My friends were the most important thing in the world to me, and I really stuck out in the new school. I didn't look the same, or dress the same, or even sound the same. I wasn't making new friends. I felt like a slug on the ground that everyone was grossed out by. Because I had known my old friends since kindergarten, I didn't really think that making new friends was a skill. I had to think about what I thought made a good friend. I had to think about what a friend really is. Then I had to act like a good friend, and do what a good friend would do.

"There was this other girl, Marla, who seemed like she had no friends. I didn't think I would like her at first, but I decided to make the first move and sit next to her at lunch and talk. She was shy at first, but she had moved around a lot and had lived in a lot of interesting places. She had amazing stories and was smart. I helped her go shopping, because she was even more clueless than I was about fashion. We both thought that being obsessed with fashion was dumb, but we had fun doing it. Then I asked her to sleep over one weekend. We've been like best friends ever since.

"Marla and I noticed there was another girl who nobody ever talked to, and although we weren't sure if we wanted her in our new inner circle, we felt like reaching out to her, which we did. It turns out she is a really good photographer, and so is her dad, and she knows about lights and stuff, so she took amazing pictures of us that made us feel like celebrities. Her dad has an amazing collection of old horror films. He really knows a lot about films. We've watched a couple, but I like new films better. Then the next week, her dad was invited to a special test screening and could bring all of us, so we all got to see a movie that hadn't even been released yet.

"I realize that friends are really important to me, and that, if I want to have a group of friends, I have to do something to make that happen. I'm glad I did."

Tia's Story

"I was a comparison junkie. Literally. I could tell you who was skinnier than me, taller than me, who had a smaller nose, thicker lips, shinier hair, longer legs, less hairy arms. I was always plucking hair from someplace I didn't think it should be. Wherever I went, even standing in line at a movie, I was comparing myself to a total stranger. I was usually losing the comparison game with somebody who didn't even know I existed!

"I knew it was lame, but I couldn't stop. When I did my Circle of Life, I literally had to do one whole circle just dealing with my body image. Head to toe, I had to get it out on paper all the things I thought were wrong.

"I wasn't going to show my Circle to anybody, because I was ashamed, but my friend saw it in my room and asked me about it, so I explained what I felt. I couldn't believe it, but she said she felt the same way, although I thought she was perfect. She hated her stomach and her "outie" belly button. She thought her ankles were too fat; she thought her ears stuck out too far. We showed our circles to another friend, and she had a list of everything she thought was wrong with her, and we were amazed, because we never noticed any of that stuff that she had on her list. We all ended up howling for hours, because we couldn't believe how silly all this stuff was—and it had taken up so much energy. In the end we all made a pact not to compare or judge ourselves for thirty days. I am really grateful to the Circle of Life to get me off the treadmill of endless self-judgment."

Common Teen Slices

Here is a typical list of the slices that most teens find relevant. Feel free to add any that are specific to your life. Read Chapter Three, which explains the slices in more detail along with the kinds of issues that may be relevant to each slice, to get your thinking going.

Sleeping

Eating

Exercise

Relaxation / Stress Management

Physical Health

Body Image

Self-Esteem (How do I feel about myself?)

Identity (Who do I think I am?)

Mental Health

Hobbies

Friendships

Family Relationships

Significant Others (boyfriends, girlfriends)

Spirituality

Goals / Dreams / Aspirations

Finances

Job

School / Training

Pets

Home / Personal Space

Activities: Sports / Dance / Music

Planning for the Future

Teen Circle of Life

Name _____

Date _____

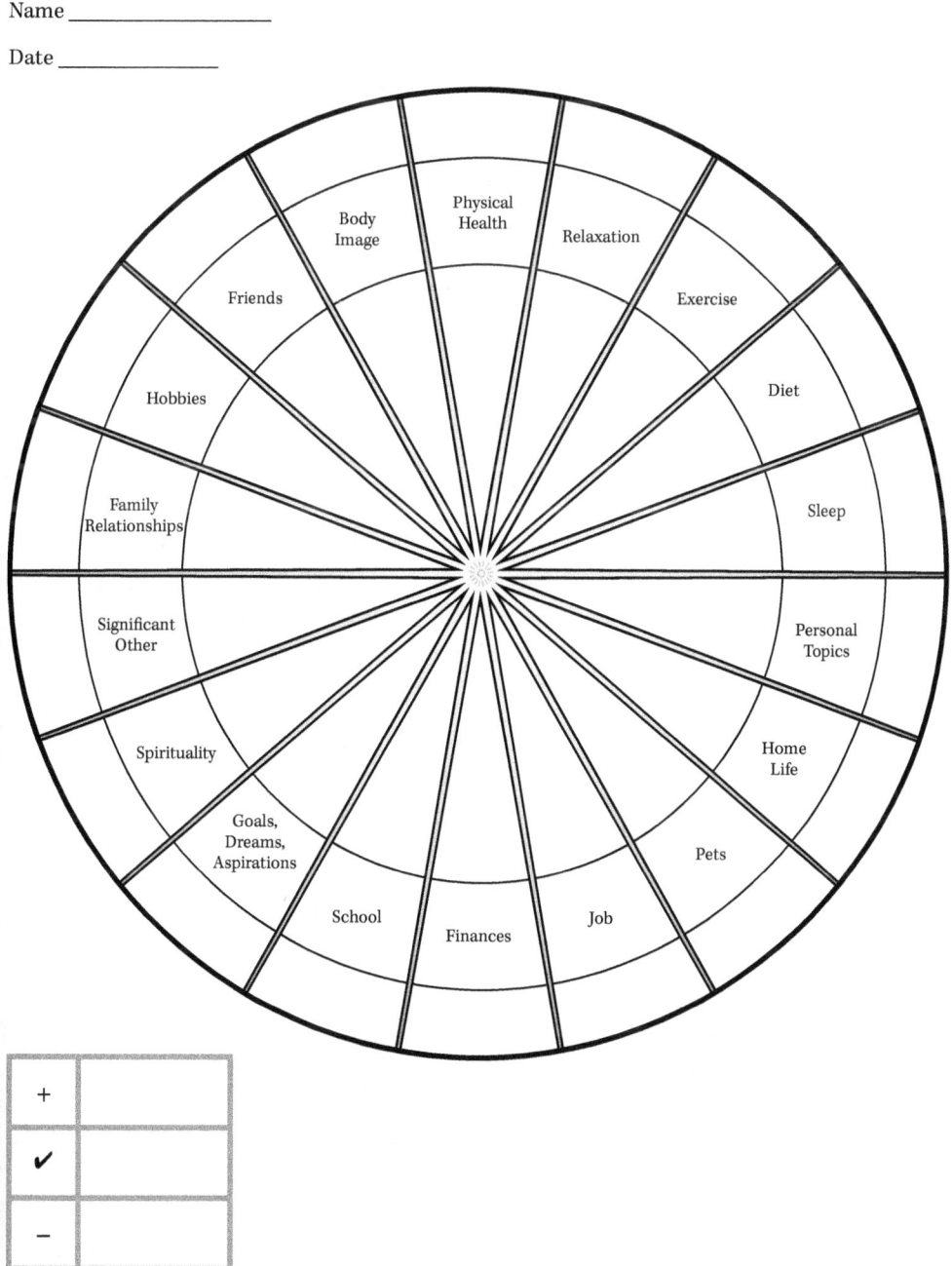

+	
✔	
−	

CHAPTER 16

Spirituality and Your Relationship to the Universe

In the Spirituality slice you are looking at your personal relationship to the universe. It's the core of what you believe about life. For some people this may be organized around their religious beliefs and affiliations. Whether or not you are connected to a particular religion, I want you to be very specific here about your personal version, about the beliefs that form the core of your relationship to how life is.

Start by seeing if you can summarize your basic beliefs about life. For example, do you believe life is fair? Do you believe that what happens to you is a matter of fate, luck, or personal decision? Do you believe in the Golden Rule? Do you believe in Karma (the idea that "What goes around comes around")? You may have different words to explain these ideas. In this step of your Circle of Life process, you want to articulate your personal sense of how the universe operates.

This is also where you look at your own ethical principles. What are the operating principles that guide your behavior?

It can be very empowering to make this a conscious process, and if you haven't done it before it can be eye opening. For example, maybe you have a belief that people should be kind to each other. This will influence how you treat others and the choices you make.

Where it can get tricky is when you encounter people who don't share these same values. You may find that they disappoint, betray, confuse, or anger you, and they may not even be aware that they have stepped on one of your ethical boundaries. Owning your own "rules of being human" can greatly reduce the amount of suffering you experience in dealing with others who don't share your values. It is not a good idea to assume or expect that they will have the same values or automatically honor yours.

Another benefit of taking the time to articulate the rules of your life's road is that it mitigates the feeling of being rudderless. Many people (of all ages) feel a certain lack of guiding spiritual principles because they may have separated themselves from their religious upbringing without articulating their own way. This step in the process can help you design your own belief structures in accordance with your heart's desires.

This is where you declare by which principles you want your life to be guided. Perhaps you are lining up with a long tradition of beliefs and values; perhaps you are creating your own. What is important is that you choose the ideas that give you a blueprint for living.

The truth is you have principles already. They just may have felt invisible if you haven't done a process of examination before. Visible or otherwise, they are still operating in your life. They affect the choices you make in every area, the friends you choose, the words you use, and the decisions you make every day.

It is an important step in maturing your life and building your character to recognize your guiding principles, because they operate at every moment. This can be very useful when you are faced with the inevitable shifts in life that come your way. What you truly believe in influences how you talk to yourself about these changes. What you believe inside will be pivotal in helping you to move forward through challenging periods.

Spirituality is very important, so take your time to focus on this slice. Once you understand your deeper values and beliefs (perhaps separating yours from those of your parents or partners), you can operate more from your core values as you make your choices in life. Understanding your own values will give you more compassion about your own life, about the choices you have made and still need to make, and give you invaluable insight into how to live your life from this day forward.

Maria's Story

When Maria came into therapy, she was feeling ambivalent about continuing to live. Her two daughters, ages 19 and 23, were off on their own, and she was feeling that she had nothing to live for. Her Circle of Life had two pluses, three checks, and thirteen minuses.

So we started with her three positive check marks, which were spirituality, hobbies, and her garden. The reason they were only checks and not pluses is because each of them felt like they were "in the gutter," as she put it. For example, she considered herself a very spiritual person; however, she had lost interest in her church over the years and stopped going.

She loved gardening, and teaching kids how to plant simple gardens, but she just wasn't spending any time teaching, and her garden was showing signs of neglect.

We decided not to focus on her thirteen minuses just yet, because they made her feel defeated and hopeless even before she began. They didn't even motivate her to take action, because the problems seemed so overwhelming. Instead, I asked her to focus on the areas that were sort of positive, but not fully functioning. I asked her what action steps she would be willing to take in these areas that genuinely made her excited when she thought about them.

Maria's first action step was to visit one new church a week within walking distance of her house (there were five). The first three were not good matches, but four and five were both promising, so she decided to visit the last two at least three times to help her make the decision about where she would choose to plant her roots. It was that fifth church that made her feel most at home and welcome. When she told the minister's wife that she liked to teach children how to garden, a "field" trip was promptly planned for their Sunday school kids.

Knowing the kids were coming in three weeks got her very motivated and excited about getting her garden, which had always been one of her great joys, into the best shape possible. The kids came and had a wonderful time planting their 12-by-12-inch gardens. The kids told their teachers at their regular school about their gardening project, and soon she had two more groups planning to visit on a Saturday.

Three months later, she was giving regular gardening classes on Saturdays, and even began private lessons with three of the most promising "green-minded" youngsters. Their enthusiasm fueled Maria's, and soon she had the energy to address some of the deeper issues in her life. She had made a few new friends from this venture, and they invited her to give a talk about children and gardening at a local Rotary Club. Her new friends gave her a renewed sense of connection and provided invaluable stimulation and camaraderie.

"I just realized this morning, when I was working in my garden," she said, "that I'm happy again. It was as if *I* had been gone for so long, I didn't even realize I was missing!"

As her garden and her circle of loving children and friends grew, Maria's life blossomed in so many unexpected ways it was a joy to watch. She began this life-changing process by just recognizing how important spirituality was in her life, and acknowledging the "hole" its absence was causing. Filling in that hole allowed her life to blossom. This shows that attending to one important area can positively impact your entire life.

Six months later, when she re-did her Circle of Life, she had 8 pluses, 5 checks, and 5 minuses. She felt so good about her ability to change the areas that needed change (her plan was to have only pluses and checks within two years), that she was able to be calm and proactive about the remaining minuses.

CHAPTER 17

The Life Review Circle

It is so important to acknowledge what you have already achieved in your life. This is not something you should just do as you stand at the end of your life. This is something you could do at any important moment. It is great to do it yearly or even more often if you are accomplishing your goals or feel you have shifted into another phase of your life. It is one way to acknowledge what you have already achieved, and that gives you the fuel to continue. It is the source of your inspiration to achieve even more.

As you think about what you would like to include in the next phase of your life, take a good look at what brings you happiness and make a plan to include that even more in your life. Focus on your core strengths and make sure you have ways to express them in the world, so that you will find greater satisfaction and perhaps significantly contribute to the happiness of others. Make a vow to reduce spending time on activities that don't result in a positive return.

As mentioned earlier, for more information on understanding your signature strengths, visit www.authentichappiness.org, where there are a number of quizzes you can take for free. Also, read books by Martin Seligman, Ph.D. (see bibliography), who has written extensively on the topic.

As you move into a life by design, you want to increase the sense of flow and ease in your world. You are also looking to spend more time with the people, places, and activities that you find meaningful. You want to make sure you are living your life with as much creativity as feels good to you.

Five Tips to Living a Meaningful Life

Creativity

Creativity goes beyond the obvious production of works of art. Creativity is an approach to living where you think of novel and productive ways to live and do all things in your daily life.

Curiosity

You want to take your curiosity seriously! Explore those people, places, and things that intrigue you. Focus on what you find fascinating! Make new discoveries about the world around you.

Lifelong Learning

Learn something new, and cultivate a love of learning. Learning anything new, physical or mental, keeps the brain sharp. Mastering new skills makes new connectivity in the brain. So take that ballroom dance class, or that computer class, or that language course, or painting with water colors, or playing the guitar, or that acting class, or creative writing—whatever inspires you to expand your vistas.

Cultivate Positivity

Deliberately focus on positivity. Recall pleasant emotions and experiences, and use these positive memories as an emotional bank account that you can draw on. Savor the everyday pleasures of life and cultivate happiness all the time. Consider taking up meditation. Experiencing inner peace and joy will make you more positive about yourself and the world around you. It can truly help you reorient your mind in a positive direction.

Engage and Contribute

Seek ways to contribute to the lives of others. Focusing on helping or mentoring others is the best way to improve your own sense of well-being. It gets you thinking about something greater than your own world and widens your perspectives on living. Getting engaged with others is essential for your happiness. Living a meaningful life is the best protection for mental health!

Filling Your Tanks with Positive Energy

As mentioned before, Dr. John Gray (author of more than a dozen best-selling books, including *Men are from Mars, Women are from Venus*) is a great resource for understanding love, life, and relationships. I have borrowed some of his ideas that he called "Love Tanks" and applied them to the slices in the Circle of Life. He uses the analogy of a tank being empty or filled to refer to the different aspects of love that we need in our life to feel balanced and whole. An imbalance in one specific slice can affect many areas of your life.

In John Gray's book titled *How to Get What You Want and Want What You Have*, he explains this idea of love tanks in great detail. He looks at this from the perspective of developmental life phases, suggesting that there are certain stages in our life that are optimal to fill these tanks and that, if they don't get filled, those effects can show up as deficiencies at other times in our life. He talks about how to fill or re-fill empty tanks. It can be a useful tool to see where you are feeling deficient, and you can then begin to address this imbalance.

Here is a brief overview of the Love Tanks

Tank One is about receiving love and support from God. From conception to birth is when this tank is filled.

Tank Two has to do with parental love. Your parents are the most significant people in your life from birth through age 7. This is the time to learn to trust and to feel safe in the world. If your parental tank is empty, or you didn't have a very good childhood experience, you may still feel that you are missing that experience of having love and trust in your life and you might be trying to get your partner to fill that sense of emptiness. Yet this is asking too much, because your partner can never fill your parental love tank. The love you experience with a partner is a different kind of love from this parental love tank. Know that you can heal this part of yourself, and do not try to get your partner to fill this void.

Tank Three refers to the love from friends and family and through the pursuit of fun activities.

Tank Four relates to peer support, appreciation, and contact with others your age.

Tank Five deals with self-love and exploring and expanding your full potential. If this tank is empty, it's hard to believe that someone loves you.

Tank Six deals with love, romance, and relationships. Filling this tank can also help with other areas of your life, such as work and productivity.

Tank Seven is the unconditional love of caring for others, such as children and pets.

Tank Eight is when you give back to your local community.

Tank Nine is where you feel a greater connection to humanity and you have a desire to give back to the world at large.

Tank Ten is about achieving full adult maturity and serving God or your deepest spiritual principles.

The Love Tanks and Your Circle of Life

These ten Love Tanks relate to the slices in the Circle of Life review, because we need all our tanks to be reasonably filled in order for our life to feel balanced and harmonious. When one tank is very low, it affects all aspects of our life. Sometimes people get stuck at one stage or another and have trouble moving forward to the next developmental stage. For example, think about a thirty-two-year-old still hanging out with his high school buddies and letting his parents pay for his

Life Review Circle

Name ____________________

Date ________________

Age ______

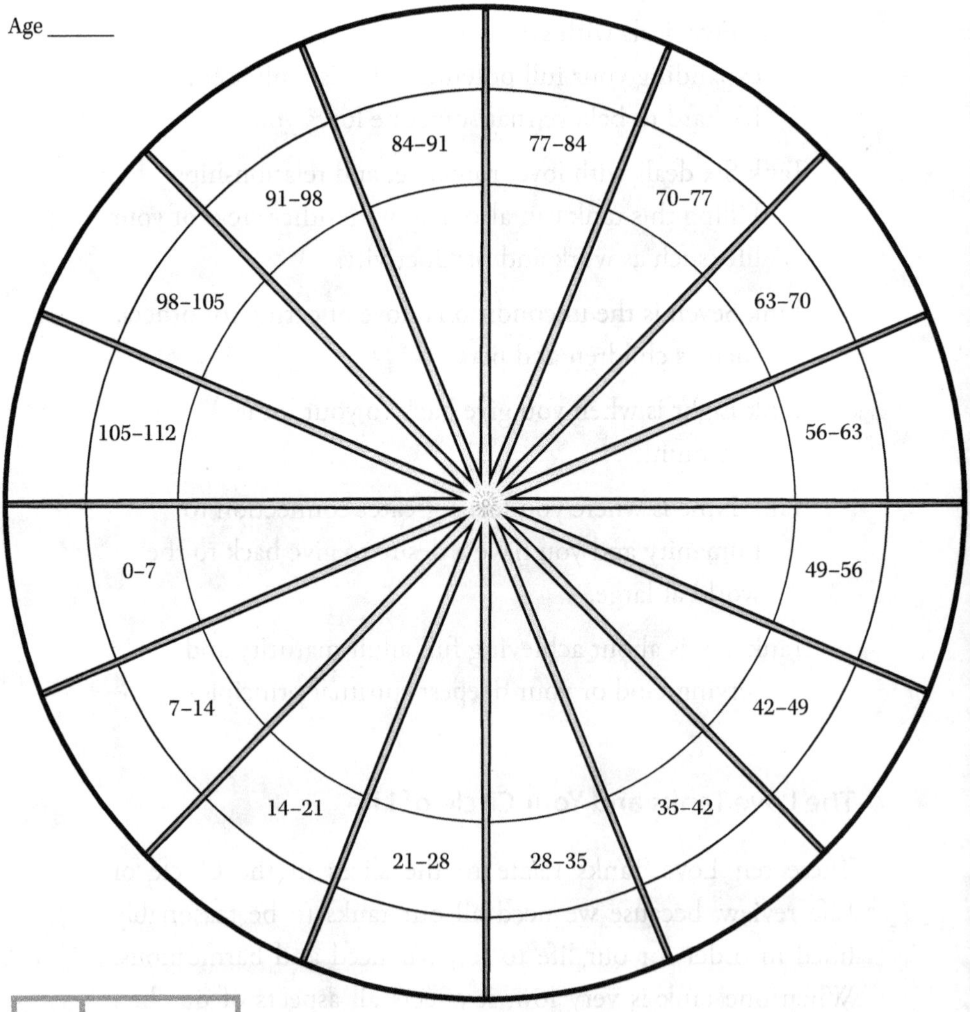
84–91
77–84
91–98
70–77
98–105
63–70
105–112
56–63
0–7
49–56
7–14
42–49
14–21
35–42
21–28
28–35

+	
✓	
–	

car insurance. Identifying which tank needs filling is half the battle right there! Often people literally are seeking love from all the wrong tanks.

Sometimes, if people have missed a love tank experience, they feel they need to go back and get that experience. This is commonly labeled as a "mid-life crisis"; however, it can happen at any age. It helps to understand what the real need is, and then to address it in ways that don't disrupt your adult life.

When you do a Life Review Circle, you are looking at this whole issue from a bird's-eye perspective on your whole life. It is a wonderful and productive thing to do such a circle. Do it at any point when you feel you could benefit from a sense of perspective. For the Life Review Circle, you are going to make a circle using the phases of life as your slices.

I have modified John Gray's concept of the Love Tanks and put them into the form of slices so you can use them in your Life Review Circle. What follows are some suggested ideas for Life Review Slices. Feel free to modify them if there are more significant categories for your particular life. These examples of slices and questions are designed to get your own thoughts going. They are by no means definitive, so do modify them in order to reflect important periods in your life more accurately.

It is important to remember that there is no one-size-fits-all formula for how your life should unfold. Everyone's life cycle is unique. What follows is a description of what the optimal life stages might include. Use it as a guide to see how your life has evolved and to give you insight into areas you may need to strengthen or heal. Some areas may give you great satisfaction, while others may need some attention.

Even if you didn't get what you needed during these stages of development, as an adult you can begin systematically to strengthen specific areas. It is never too late to heal even childhood wounds. Understanding what specific stage of your life was unfulfilled will assist you in your process of getting those needs met.

Life Review Slices

Early Childhood

Was your mother present, nurturing, and available? Were you breast-fed? Were you supported by your father? Was he present? Did you feel loved and cared for? Were your parents present for important moments in your life? Did you feel a sense of trust that they would be there for you? Were there other siblings present? How did they respond to your entry into the family? Or how did you respond to new siblings or step-siblings in your family?

Later Childhood

What was your childhood like? Did you feel loved and protected? Do you remember your childhood? What feelings did you have? Were you happy? Did you have friends you could play with and have fun? What do you remember about your childhood? Do you still see friends from childhood?

Adolescence

How was your adolescence? What do you remember about your teen years? Were you happy or not? How was your introduction to dating and intimacy? How did you get along with your peers? Did you have close friends? Are any of these friends still present in your life today? How were your high school years? Did you get good grades? Have good friends?

Were you active in extra-curricular activities and hobbies? Did you participate in sports? How was your self-esteem? If you moved from your parent's house, when did you move? Where did you move to? What did you do after high school? Did you work? Did you go to college?

Developing Your Adult Self

How did you feel about your sense of self in the world? How did you feel about being an adult? What did you think about being an adult? What did you want in your life? Did you have a sense of your purpose? Did you go to college? Did you work? Did you feel you got to explore the possibilities that were meaningful to you? Did you feel you got to expand and unfold your personal potential and see things from your own unique point of view? This was an ideal time to develop your self-concept. If you can remember your self-talk at the time, it will give you a clue to how you felt about yourself.

Forming a Partnership and/or Developing Your Career

What were your adult intimate relationships like? Whom were you attracted to? What were their characteristics or qualities? Did you learn how to be a partner in a relationship? Did you have a few or many relationships? How did you feel being in a relationship? Did you marry? Did you focus on a job or career?

Giving Love to Those Close to You

Did you have children or pets or people who depended on you? Were you able to love others without feeling resentment or feeling overwhelmed? How did you feel about how your life was moving forward? What kind of people were in your life?

Connecting to Your Community

Do you feel you have a place in the world? Do you have a community or people around you that you feel connected to? Do you consider yourself a member of a community? Do you feel isolated or alone? Do you do anything to give back to your community? Do you feel on track with your purpose?

Giving Love and Serving the World:

Do you feel connected to humanity and important causes in your world? Do you feel your life has meaning? Are you accomplishing what you wish to accomplish? Are you traveling and enjoying seeing the world around you?

Self Mastery

Self Mastery means defining life by your own terms . . . flowing and enjoying life and trusting yourself and your sense of truth . . . supporting others to be the best they can be.

If your life would benefit by a different division of phases or ages, feel free to adjust the slices according to your personal life segments. If, for example, you are doing a life review at age thirty-five, you might want to adjust your life into one slice for every five, seven, or nine years. You could use this as a vision map for where you want to be in later years.

Balance of Motion and the Natural Rhythms of Life

The great thing about having a total perspective on your life is the realization that there are phases of life in which different issues are important to you. For example, there are some segments of your life where your focus is strongly on achievement and moving forward. Then there are other phases where the emphasis is on the moment. This is a phase of enjoying what you have without always worrying about moving ahead. Understanding your natural life rhythms of movement and the pleasure of stillness can allow you to have more gratitude for the particular phase in which you are living.

Ultimately, the secret to a happy life is to cultivate a healthy balance between moving forward and enjoying the present. Balance is an art because it means alternating our energy patterns. We can't always be striving or moving and even pushing forward. We also need to be able to take a moment and enjoy and be grateful for what we already have accomplished by acknowledging all the good we have already done.

Doing a Life Review Circle should absolutely include taking stock of all the things you have accomplished in your life. This is like stoking the fire. It's okay to pat yourself on the back. It gives you more energy to proceed if you take a moment to smell the roses of your life, meaning all that is good and all that is working.

As you look at your Life Review Circle, recall what happened during those phases. What themes were important in these different slices of time? Contemplate the lessons learned that helped you as you moved forward into the next phase of your life.

One method is to focus on the goals or challenges you had at the time, or the people who were important in your life.

Zero in and reflect on these different phases or seasons of your life. What do you notice about these different cycles? What thoughts, feelings, goals, activities, or dreams were important to you? What has changed? What is different for you now? Where do you want to go next?

By scoring the slices on your Life Review Circle you will be able to understand how you felt about the various phases in your life. The outer ring on the Life Review circle gives you the opportunity to make notes about your experiences with your life so far. You may write about the life lesson's you've learned or the meaning you've gained from past events. Also, you may choose to recall a significant event and decide that you would like to heal this past experience by forgiving someone or yourself for what happened. This could be your time to let yourself fully embrace your past with understanding, compassion and gratitude. To learn how to heal the past by writing a feeling letter please refer to Dr. John Gray's book, *Men are from Mars Women are from Venus* (pages 206–245).

At each stage in your life there is the possibility of redirecting your energy and focus. This is so that you can move toward where you want to go.

Explore Gratitude

Doing a Life Review Circle is the perfect opportunity to explore gratitude. Gratitude has many benefits such as increasing optimism, better health, and motivation for you to continue to achieve your goals. For all those reasons, this is a great time to continue or begin to explore gratitude for your life. Your life is unique. No one else has lived exactly like you. You may be amazed at the people who have been part of your life and the variety of experiences you have had. Take in the unique beauty of the life you have created. Even the negative experiences made you stronger, helped you in making decisions, and increased your knowledge and wisdom. The more you focus on gratitude, the more you bring it into your life.

Just knowing you have the power to create your life will inspire you to make conscious choices that lead you to more joy, wisdom, and happiness.

Write down all the people in your life that you are grateful for and how and why they have contributed to your life. Dr. Seligman, in *Authentic Happiness*, recommends keeping a gratitude journal that you can write in every night before you go to bed. Take a moment to reflect on what you are grateful for during the day. If there are people involved, or situations and experiences that you feel grateful for, write them down in detail. Several studies show that if you experience more gratefulness your mind starts identifying more things you can feel grateful for. This opens you up and draws you to more ways that you have to feel grateful, and this leads to a greater feeling of well being and optimism.

It's Never Too Late to Have a Happy Childhood

This is a wonderful expression. What it means is that, no matter what happened—or didn't happen—in your formative years, you can still heal yourself and make good decisions and be happy for the rest of your life.

The Gratitude Circle

As a creative option, you could make a circle of the most important people in your life—those who have loved and supported you, and those you have loved. You could name it your Circle of Gratitude and list a person in each slice with whom you feel connected. When you finish your circle, you will have a visual reminder of the special people in your life, and you can draw on those connections when you feel down or alone or disconnected.

See my Circle of Gratitude in the acknowledgments section of this book.

It is always a perfect time to do a Circle of Life review. It is taking a moment away from the routine, away from the emergencies and the endless details of daily life. This is where you look over your Circle and see its perfection, or acknowledge that it needs some correction. This is how you lead a life by design instead of by accident. This is how you become the master builder of all your dreams.

Imagine if you could be transported to the last years of your life—with the wisdom that perspective brings. Imagine that you had learned your lessons and you were no longer "sweating the small stuff." Imagine that you now have the wisdom and perspective you have gained from doing your Complete Life Circle.

With this perspective in mind, here are two questions for you to contemplate:

1. If you knew your time was limited, how would you live your life differently?
2. Why not begin to live it that way now?

Stella's Story

Stella was seventy-seven when she sat down to begin her Life Review Circle. She had had what she called a "colorful life," with many twists and turns. It wasn't until she took the time to do a Life Review Circle that she truly began to appreciate how purposeful and non-random her life had been. She chose to use seven-year cycles to create her slices. Once she saw her whole life on one page, it gave her tremendous appreciation for all that she had experienced. Instead of spending time regretting choices she had made, she was able to see for the first time how everything that had happened had made her the strong person she had become.

Stella felt her early childhood years were happy and stable, but her adult years were more challenging. Her career as a rising executive assistant was cut short by having a child as a single mother at age 26. She did her best as a single mom to raise her daughter. She began to get her executive career back on track when her daughter was five. When her daughter was eighteen, the daughter got into drugs and married a man who was incarcerated. These choices tore her and her daughter apart.

Stella's career began to take off, and she was married for the first time at age 47 to a man she had met through work a few years earlier. They loved nature and hiked together every Sunday. They became active on the board of a nature group and volunteered their time to protect the local trails. He was the love of her life, but after 22 years of happy marriage he passed away of a heart attack. Stella was alone again. Thankfully, it was at this time that she and her daughter reunited, and she was delighted to learn that she was a grandmother!

Stella loved being a grandmother; as a result, she and her daughter experienced a new closeness through the love of her seven-year-old granddaughter. In addition to playing a major part in her granddaughter's life, Stella began taking workshops in holistic health care and exercise. She took up watercolor painting for the first time, and even her classmates thought she was a natural artist.

As Stella became clearer about what was important in her own life and what was less so, she began to feel calmer and more authentic. In this commitment to her truth she became a very positive role model for both her daughter and her granddaughter. Doing the Life Review Circle helped her realize who she really was and what mattered to her the most. She made a list of all the wonderful goals she had, and felt very relaxed about achieving them. "I'm happier now than I've ever been," Stella said.

Felicity's Story

Felicity felt overwhelmed and stressed. Her life felt overcrowded, with her fulltime job at a community agency, her membership on two community boards, and her finishing her master's degree online. For her dream project, she was applying for a grant to start a charter school focused on indigenous arts and music. Everything she was doing felt important, and she believed that it could have a beneficial social impact. She didn't feel like she could let go of any one of her commitments, while the problem was that each one of these endeavors was more than a fulltime job.

"I have enough meaning for five lifetimes," she said. "I just don't have a clue how to lighten up." Her body was starting to show signs of the stress, and she was filled with mysterious pains. She was, as she put it, "burning the candle at four ends." She realized at some level she was sending out a message to the universe to "slow down" because, even though she wasn't ready to admit it, she needed a break. She realized she needed to do less and focus on her health. If she hadn't recognized this when she did, she might have developed a major physical illness to force her to slow down. Fortunately, she realized the unconscious message she was sending out, because she wanted to slow down and didn't want to have to go through the process of a lengthy and unknown illness, as she had done in her college years.

Felicity's problem was that every area of her life felt like a priority. None of them were getting her best energy, because she was just stretched too thin. In doing her Circle of Life, she realized she had this image of herself as someone who had to make the world a better place. This was an idea she liked, but it was ruining her own life. She realized that she had to put her personal life on track before she could refocus on the rest of her life.

She took time to complete a Circle of Life review. As she examined the phases of her life, she realized what she needed to do to make her life work better. She spent some time thinking about her strengths and greatest joys. That led her to come up with a priority list that involved phasing out her work on the two boards in the next six months, and putting all her attention on finishing her degree and doing well at her paid job. Then she could begin by adding one thing back, her grant work for the development of the charter school. At the end of this Life Review process, she felt clear about what she needed to do.

Letting go of having to be "superwoman" eased the load of mental and physical strain. Once she stopped trying to save the world, her body began to recover, and she had more energy for the people and tasks that were right in front of her. She began to feel more effective and inspired, realizing that she could have all her dreams, just not all of them today.

Conclusion

*I*t has been deeply fulfilling to see how transformative the Circle of Life process has been for so many patients, family members, and friends. The process has evolved over the decades. What began as a simple exercise of delineating the aspects of one's life became a method to create a life by design.

It all begins with the first steps of the process, when you check in with yourself in present time and assess how you are doing in the various areas of your life. Then you move on to contemplate what you would like to see accomplished. Next, you imagine and set your intention on this new outcome and prepare to follow through.

My patients have created multiple circles at different periods in their lives as well as, for various reasons (dating, marriage, new career, having a child, etc.) It became obvious that what was being created was an evolving spiral of ongoing adjustments and fine tuning of their life journeys. It is not a static process. It is alive and growing and changing, as the participants are willing to consider new options and choices.

It is a wonderful process to see in action, starting with the first steps of going around the Circle of Life and filling in each slice and then assessing your score. It always amazes me that the scores patients end up with are such an accurate reflection of their true sense about their life.

Once you decide what you are willing to do to enhance the quality of your life, you are usually motivated and can clearly see the areas and the possibilities to make changes. Once you fill in the outer circle with new activities, then it is time to let go and get into a relaxed, meditative state and imagine these changes already easily and naturally occurring. I find that patients enjoy taking time to relax into accepting these new changes. Busyness and pushing oneself aren't always the best strategy for making authentic changes. Sometimes you have to let go and flow, and let the changes happen.

Next you complete your Circle of Goals. This is something you want to put some place where you will see it frequently. You will be able to see your progress as well as be reminded of where you need to continue your focus. This phase sets the course for your new direction.

Over time, if you save your circles, you will see your journey and those of your partners, and you can build on the knowledge that change and growth happen and will continue if you nurture them. Whether it's just to see your life more clearly, or to use the Circle of Life process as a tool throughout your life, I hope you will enjoy it.

Just remember that it requires work and application on your part. It is worth it, because your life can unfold beautifully for you if you are willing to help it along.

If you're interested in pursuing your own Circles of Life you can go to the webpage www.drmitzigold.com and download Circles of your choice.

Please direct all inquiries to
info@drmitzigold.com

Recommended Reading and Further Resources

Anderson, R. (1976). *SHE: Understanding Feminine Psychology.* King of Prussia, PA: Religious Publishing Co.

Arguelles, J. (1972). *Mandala* Boulder Co: Shambala Publishing

Arrien, A. (1993). *The Four-Fold Way: Walking the Path of the Warrior, Teacher, Healer, and Visionary.* New York, NY: HarperCollins.

Balch, P. (2010). *Prescription for Nutritional Healing.* New York, NY: Penguin Group.

Batmanghelidj, F. (1999). *Your Body's Many Cries for Water.* Falls Church, VA: Global Health Solutions.

Benton, D. A. (1992). *Lions Don't Need to Roar.* New York, NY: Warner Brothers.

Bloomfield, H., & Goldberg, P. (2000). *Making Peace with Your Past.* New York, NY: HarperCollins.

Bloomfield, H. H. (1988). *Healing Anxiety with Herbs.* New York, NY: HarperCollins.

Bolen, J. (1979). *The Tao of Psychology: The Synchronicity and the Self.* New York, NY: Harper & Row.

Bolen, J. S. (1989). *God's in Every Man.* New York, NY: Harper & Row.

Bolen, J. S. (1999). *The Millionth Circle.* San Francisco, CA: Conari Press.

Boston Women's Health Book Collective (1992). *Our Bodies, Ourselves.* New York, NY: Touchstone Publishing.

Branden, N. (1980). *The Psychology of Romantic Love.* New York, NY: Penguin Group.

Branden, N. (1985). *If You Could Hear What I Cannot Say.* New York, NY: Bantam Publishing.

Branden, N. (1985). *To See What I See and Know What I Want.* New York, NY: Bantam Publishing.

Branden, N. (1992). *The Power of Self-Esteem.* Space Deerfield Beach, FL: Health Communications.

Branden, N. (1995). *Six Pillars of Self-Esteem.* New York, NY: Bantam Publishing.

Braverman, E. (2006). *The Edge Effect.* New York, NY: Sterling Publishing Co.

Brennan, B. (1999). *Seeds of the Spirit.* Boca Raton, FL: Barbara Brennan.

Bronson, P. O. (2002). *What Should I Do with My Life?* New York, NY: Random House.

Butler, P. (1991). *Talking to Yourself: Learning the Language of Self Affirmations.* New York, NY: HarperCollins.

Campbell, J. (2007). *The Mythic Dimension*. Novado CA: New World Library.

Campbell, J. (2008) *The Hero with a Thousand Faces*. Novado CA: New World Library.

Chatman, G. (1992). *The 5 Love Languages*. Chicago, IL: Northfield Publishing.

Childre, D., & Paddison, S. (1998*). Heart Math Discovery Program*. Boulder Creek, CA: Planetary Publications.

Chiang, H., & Maslow, A. (1977). *The Healthy Personality*. Princeton, NJ: D. Van Nostrand.

Chopra, D. (1993). *Ageless Body, Timeless Mind*. New York, NY: Harmony Books.

Coates, B. A. (2008). *Divorce with Decency: The Complete How-To Book and Survivors Guide to the Legal, Emotional, Economic and Social Issues*. Honolulu, HI: University of Hawaii Press.

Covey, S. (1989). *The 7 Habits of Highly Effective People*. New York, NY: Simon & Schuster.

Csikszentmihalyi, M. (1990). *Flow*. New York, NY: HarperCollins.

Csikszentminalyi, M. (1993). *The Evolving Self*. New York, NY: HarperCollins.

D'Adamo, P., & Whitney, C. (1996). *Eat Right 4 Your Type: The Individualized Diet Solution to Staying Healthy, Living Longer, Achieving Your Ideal Weight*. New York, NY: Putnam.

D'Adamo, P., & Whitney, C. (2001). *Live Right 4 Your Type*. New York, NY: Putnam.

D'Adamo, P., & Whitney, C. (2007). *The Genotype Diet.* New York, NY: Broadway Books.

Dyer, W. (2004). *The Power of Intention.* Carlsbad, CA: Hay House Publishing.

Ellis, A. (2005) *The Myth of Self Esteem: How Rational Emotive Behavior Therapy Can Change Your Life Forever.* Amherst, NY: Prometheus Books.

Emoto, M. (1999). *Messages from Water.* Torrance, CA: Hado Publishing.

Fallon, S., & Enig, G. M. (2001). *Nourishing Traditions.* Washington, DC: Newtrends Publishing.

Feinstein, D., and Krippner, S. (1989). *Personal Mythology: Using Dreams, Rituals, and Imagination to Discover Your Inner Story.* Los Angeles, CA: Jeremy P. Tarcher.

Feldhahn, S. (2004). *For Women Only.* New York, NY: Multnomah.

Feldhahn, S., & Feldhahn, J. (2006). *For Men Only.* New York, NY: Multnomah.

Fisher, R. (1990). *The Knights and Rusty Armor.* Chatsworth, CA: Wilshire Book Company.

Ford, D. (1998). *The Dark Side of the Light Chasers.* New York, NY: Riverhead Trade, NY: Berkeley Books.

Ford, D. (2006). *Spiritual Divorce: Divorce as a Catalyst for an Extraordinary Life.* New York, NY: HarperCollins.

Gilligan, C. (2002). *The Birth of Pleasure.* New York, NY: Random House.

Glenn, H. S., & Nelsen, J. (1988). *Raising Self-reliant Children in a Self-indulgent World.* Rockland, CA: Prime Publishing and Communication.

Goldman, R., Klatz, R., & Berger, L. (1999). *Brain Fitness.* New York, NY: Doubleday.

Gould, R. (1978). *Transformations: Growth and Change in Adult Life.* New York, NY: Simon & Schuster.

Gray, J. (1992) *Men Are From Mars—Women Are From Venus.* New York NY HarperCollins.

Gray, J. (2010). *Venus on Fire—Mars on Ice.* Coquitlam, BC: Mind Publishing.

Gray, J. (1984). *What You Feel You Can Heal.* Mill Valley CA, Hart Publishing Company

Gray, J (1999) *How to Get What You Want and Want What You Have.* New York, NY HarperCollins

Gregor, C. (1983). *Working Out Together: A Complete Fitness Program for Partners.* New York, NY: Berkley Books.

Hanh, T. N. (1976). *The Miracle of Mindfulness.* Boston, MA: Beacon Press.

Harrill, E. S. (1987). *You Could Feel Good.* Houston, TX: Innerworks Publishing.

Hawkins, D. R. (2002). *Power vs. Force.* Carlsbad, CA: Hay House.

Hendrix, H. H. (1988). *Getting the Love You Want.* New York, NY: Henry Holt & Co.

Hicks, E., & Hicks, J. (2006). *The Law of Attraction.* Carlsbad, CA: Hay House.

Hope, W. A., McHale, M. S., & Craighead, E. W. (1988). *Self-esteem: Enhancement within Children and Adolescents.* New York, NY: Oxford, Pergamon Press.

Houston, J. (1996). *A Mythic Life: Learning to Live Our Greater Story.* New York, NY: HarperCollins.

Howard, V. (1965). *Psycho-Pictography: The New Way to Use the Miracle Power of Your Mind.* West Nyack, NY: Parker Publishing.

Howard, V. (1967). *Mystic Path to Cosmic Power.* West Nyack, NY: Parker Publishing.

Jeffers, S. (1987). *Feel the Fear and Do It Anyway.* New York, NY: Ballantine Books.

Jeffers, S. (1999). *In the Struggle and Dance with Life.* New York, NY: St. Martin's Press.

Johnson, A. R. (1983). *We.* San Francisco, CA: Harper & Row.

Johnson, S. (1988). *Who Moved My Cheese?* New York, NY: Putnam's Sons.

Kabat-Zinn, J. (1994). *Wherever You Go There You Are.* New York, NY: Hyperion Group.

Kasl, C. (2008). *The Buddha Got Stuck.* New York, NY: Penguin Books.

Keyes, K. (1979). *A Conscious Person's Guide to Relationships.* Coos Bay, OR: living love publications.

Kroeger, H. (1996). *New Dimensions in Healing Yourself.* Boulder, CO: Hanna Kroeger Publications.

Learner, H. (2004). *Fear and Other Uninvited Guests.* New York, NY: HarperCollins.

Leonard, S. L. (1989). *On the Way to the Wedding.* Boston, MA: Shambala Publishing, Inc.

Linley, P. A., Joseph, S., & Seligman, M. (2004). *Positive Psychology and Practice.* Hoboken, NJ: John Wiley & Sons.

McKay, M., & Fanning, P. (1992). *Self Esteem*. Oakland, CA: New Harbinger.

McWilliams, J. R., & McWilliams, P. (1991). *Do It*. Los Angeles, CA: Prelude Press.

McWilliams, P. (1994). *Life 101*. Santa Monica, CA: Prelude Press.

McTaggart, L. (2007). *The Intention Experiment: Using your Thoughts to Change Life in the World*. New York, NY: Simon & Schuster.

Merritt, C. (1999). *Finding Love (Again!)*. Wilsonville, OR: Book Partners.

Moore, T. (1994). *Soul Mates—Honoring the Mysteries of Love and Relationship*. New York, NY: Harper Perennial.

Moss, R. (1981). *The I That Is We*. Berkeley, CA: Celestial Arts.

Pearsall, P. (1994). *A Healing Intimacy: The Power of Loving Connections*. New York, NY: Three Rivers Press.

Pearson, C. (1989). *The Hero Within: Six Archetypes We Live By*. New York, NY: HarperCollins.

Peterson, C., & Seligman, M. E. P. (2004). *Character Strengths and Virtues*. New York, NY: Oxford.

Peterson, C. (2006). *A Primer and Positive Psychology*. New York, Oxford Press.

Radin, D. (2006). *Entangled Minds*. New York, NY: Paraview Pocket Books.

Raffel, L. (1997). *Should I Stay or Should I Go: How Controlled Separation Can Save Your Marriage*. Lincolnwood, IL: Contemporary Books.

Roth, G., & Loudon, J. (1989). *Maps to Ecstasy: Teachings of an Urban Shaman*. Novato, CA: New World Library.

Roundtree, C. (1991). *Coming into Your Fullness*. Freedom, CA: The Crossing Press.

Rove, M., Bloomfield, H., & McWilliams, P. (1976). *How to Survive the Loss of a Love*. New York, NY: Prelude Press.

Rowe, J., & Kahn, R. (1988). *Successful Aging*. New York, NY: Dell Publishing.

Ruiz, M. (1997). *The Four Agreements: A Practical Guide to Personal Freedom*. San Rafael, CA: Amber-Allen Publishing, Inc.

Ruiz, M., Ruiz, J., & Mills, J. (2010). *The Fifth Agreement*. San Rafael, CA: Amber-Allen Publishing.

Sandoz, B. (1997). *Parachutes for Parents: 12 New Keys to Raising Children for a Better World*. Chicago, IL: Contemporary Books.

Sapolsky, R. M. (1994). *Why Zebras Don't Get Ulcers: A Guide to Stress, Stress Related Diseases and Coping*. New York, NY: W. H. Freeman.

Schultz, D. (1977). *Gross Psychology: Models of a Healthy Personality*. New York, NY: Van Nostrand Reinhold Co.

Schlitz, M. H., Vieten, C., & Amorok, T. (2007). *Living Deeply*. Oakland, CA: New Harbinger.

Seligman, M. (2002) *Authentic Happiness*. New York, NY Free Press Simon and Schuster.

Seligman, M. (1990). *Learned Optimism: How to Change Your Mind and Your Life*. New York, NY: Pocket Books.

Seligman, M. E. (1993). *What You Can Change*. New York, NY: Random House.

Sher, B. (1979). *Witchcraft.* New York, NY: Random House.

Sher, B. (1994). *I Could Do Anything: If I Only Knew What it Was.* New York, NY: Dell Publishing.

Somers, S. (2008). *Breakthrough: Eight Steps to Wellness.* New York, NY: Crown Publishers.

Staley, B. (1988). *Between Form and Freedom: A Practical Guide to the Teenage Years.* Stroud, England: Hawthorn Press.

Steinem, G. (1993). *Revolution from Within.* Boston, MA: Little, Brown and Company.

Stevens, John. Enso(2009). *The Timeless Circle.* Robyn Buntin in Honolulu.

Sujata, A. (1980). *Beginning to See.* Santa Cruz, CA: Unity Press.

Tolle, E. (2005). *A New Earth: Awakening to Your Life's Purpose.* New York, NY: Penguin Group.

VanZant, L. (2002). *Up from Here: Reclaiming the Male Spirit: A Guide to Transforming Emotions into Power and Freedom.* New York, NY: HarperCollins.

Walsh, R., & Vaughan, F. (1976). *Beyond Ego: Transpersonal Dimensions in Psychology.* Los Angeles, CA: Tarcher.

Weil, A. (1995). *Help and Healing.* New York, NY: Houghton Mifflin.

Weil. A. (1995). *Natural Health, Natural Medicine.* New York, NY: Houghton Mifflin.

Wertheimer, M. (1979). *A Brief History of Psychology.* Orlando, FL: Holt, Rinehart and Winston, Inc.

Welwood, J. (1983). *Awakening the Heart.* Boulder, CO: Shambhala.

Welwood, J. (1990). *Journey of the Heart*. New York, NY: HarperCollins.

Whitmore, E. (1979). *The Symbolic Quest: Basic Concepts of Analytical Psychology*. Princeton, NJ: Princeton University Press.

Wilber, K. (1979). *No Boundary—Eastern and Western Approaches to Personal Growth*. Boulder, CO: Shambhala.

Williams, P. (1995). *Love 101*. Los Angeles, CA: Prelude Press.

Williams, R. M. (2004). *PSYCH-K...The Missing Peace in your Life*. Crestone, CO: Myrddin Publications.

Complete Your Own Circle of Life

Circle of Life

Name _____

Date _____

+	
✔	
−	

Balancing Your Circle of Life

Circle of Life

Name _____

Date _____

Segments (clockwise from top):
- Physical Health
- Relaxation Stress Management
- Exercise
- Diet
- Sleep
- Home
- Pets
- Education/Training
- Career/Job
- Finances
- Goals, Dreams, Aspirations
- Spirituality
- Children
- Significant Other
- Family Origin
- Friends Co-workers
- Hobbies
- Mental Health Self Esteem

+	
✔	
−	

Couples Circle of Life

Name _____   Name _____

Date _____   Date _____

Labels around the wheel:
- Physical Health
- Mental Health / Self Esteem
- Relaxation / Stress Management
- Hobbies
- Exercise
- Friends / Co-workers
- Diet
- Family Origin
- Sleep
- Significant Other
- Home
- Children
- Pets
- Spirituality
- Education/Training
- Goals, Dreams, Aspirations
- Career/Job
- Finances

+	
✔	
−	

+	
✔	
−	

Dual Couples Circle of Life

Name _____

Date _____

- Physical Health
- Mental Health / Self Esteem
- Hobbies
- Friends / Co-workers
- Family Origin
- Significant Other
- Children
- Spirituality
- Goals, Dreams, Aspirations
- Finances
- Career/Job
- Education/Training
- Pets
- Home
- Sleep
- Diet
- Exercise
- Relaxation / Stress Management

+	
✓	
−	

Draw Your Own Circle of Life **191**

Name _____

Date _____

+	
✓	
−	

Segments (clockwise from top):
- Physical Health
- Relaxation Stress Management
- Exercise
- Diet
- Sleep
- Home
- Pets
- Education/Training
- Career/Job
- Finances
- Goals, Dreams, Aspirations
- Spirituality
- Children
- Significant Other
- Family Origin
- Friends Co-workers
- Hobbies
- Mental Health Self Esteem

Teen Circle of Life

Name _____

Date _____

Wheel segments (clockwise from top):
- Physical Health
- Relaxation Stress Management
- Exercise
- Diet
- Sleep
- Home
- Pets
- Education/Training
- Career/Job
- Finances
- Goals, Dreams, Aspirations
- Spirituality
- Children
- Significant Other
- Family Origin
- Friends Co-workers
- Hobbies
- Mental Health Self Esteem

+	
✔	
−	

Draw Your Own Circle of Life   **193**

Life Review Circle

Name _____

Date _____

Age _____

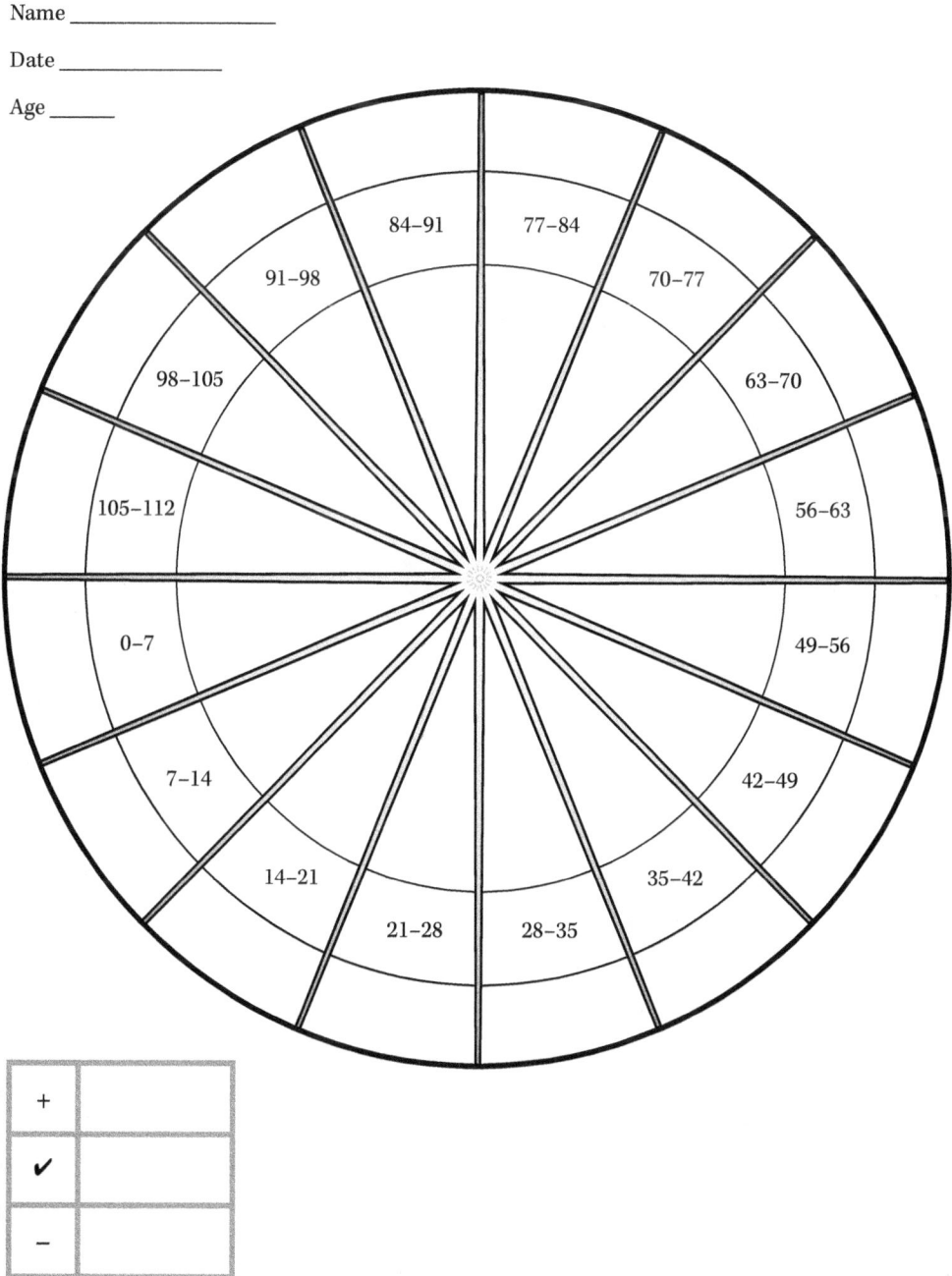

194 Balancing Your Circle of Life

About the Author

Dr. Mitzi Gold is an accomplished therapist who supports people in realizing their potential. She has been in private practice since 1982, and has expertise in the fields of mind/body/energy therapies, consciousness exploration, and integrative and complementary approaches to health.

Dr. Gold encourages her patients to discover their authentic self, and enhance their well being. She shares her background in diverse therapeutic techniques of healing and training with people who want to learn to live life fully, with passion and purpose, to positively influence the world around them.

Dr. Gold has also worked extensively with Dr. John Gray, a leading expert in the field of relationships. He is the author of "Men are from Mars, Women are from Venus," as well as many other books. Dr. Gold is the director of Hawaii's only Mars and Venus Counseling Center. An accomplished speaker and lecturer, she has conducted classes, workshops, and seminars on a wide range of topics, and has hosted her own weekly television and radio shows. She lives in Hawaii with her husband, Frank Rogers.

The Dragon

This is my Dragon. It is one of my drawings from my first Zen Brush painting class. It helped me set my intention to complete this book in my Year of the Dragon.

What's Next?

Please visit www.drmitzigold.com to find
the circle you want to download for your own use.

We'll be happy to answer your questions and
support you in using the Circle of Life process.

For Classes and workshops: info@drmitzigold.com

Book sales: To shop on the website go to
www.drmitzigold.com or call (808) 737-6277 USA.

Additional copies of the book and ebook editions can
be purchased through bookstores and online retailers.

www.ingramcontent.com/pod-product-compliance
Lightning Source LLC
Chambersburg PA
CBHW061758110426
42742CB00012BB/1937